Feminism Beyond Left and Right

Feminism Beyond Left and Right

HOLLY LAWFORD-SMITH

polity

Copyright © Holly Lawford-Smith, 2025

The Author hereby asserts her moral right to be identified as author of the Work

First published by Polity Press in 2025

Polity Press
65 Bridge Street
Cambridge CB2 1UR, UK

Polity Press
111 River Street
Hoboken, NJ 07030, USA

All rights reserved. Except for the quotation of short passages for the purpose of criticism and review, no part of this publication may be reproduced, stored in a retrieval system or transmitted, in any form or by any means, electronic, mechanical, photocopying, recording or otherwise, without the prior permission of the publisher.

ISBN-13: 978-1-5095-6479-8 – hardback
ISBN-13: 978-1-5095-6480-4 – paperback

A catalogue record for this book is available from the British Library.

Library of Congress Control Number: 2024949097

Typeset in 11 on 14pt Warnock Pro
by Cheshire Typesetting Ltd, Cuddington, Cheshire
Printed and bound in Great Britain by CPI Group (UK) Ltd, Croydon

The publisher has used its best endeavours to ensure that the URLs for external websites referred to in this book are correct and active at the time of going to press. However, the publisher has no responsibility for the websites and can make no guarantee that a site will remain live or that the content is or will remain appropriate.

Every effort has been made to trace all copyright holders, but if any have been overlooked the publisher will be pleased to include any necessary credits in any subsequent reprint or edition.

For further information on Polity, visit our website:
politybooks.com

Contents

Acknowledgements	vi
Preface	vii
1 Who Is a Feminist?	1
2 The 1960s: Feminists Leaving the Left	18
3 What's Wrong with the Right?	39
4 The Myth of Left and Right	59
5 Ethical Versus Political Reasons to Not 'Work With'	72
6 Moving Forward with Non-Partisan Feminism	103
Notes	119
References	143

Acknowledgements

I workshopped earlier versions of this manuscript at a number of universities, and I'm grateful to the audiences there for extremely helpful, constructive and thoughtful discussion: Chapman University in California, where I spent my most recent sabbatical; the University of Melbourne; and the University of Western Australia. I also gave some chapters of the book as talks at the University of Sydney and University of Melbourne, and am grateful to those audiences for their engagement. Pete Bornschein, Kate Phelan and Jen Izaakson all read the whole manuscript and gave me comments, for which I am hugely grateful. And finally, a particular thanks to Brennan McDavid, upon whom I probably inflicted the worst of my early and incoherent thoughts about this project, and who was infinitely patient and up for helping me untangle the mess.

Preface

This book, really, is an intervention on the frequent dust-ups inside feminism that happen whenever there is what a leftist might perceive as a 'right-wing threat', and to the claims routinely made in the course of those flare-ups. Let me give you a couple of examples.

In January 2019, three radical feminists and a de-transitioner (a person who previously identified as transgender) spoke on a panel titled 'The Inequality of the Equality Act: Concerns from the Left'.[1] Some British feminists flew to the United States to attend the event and support the speakers. Both the speakers and the British women were subsequently denounced for 'allying with the right'. Why? Because the *venue* for the event was the conservative think tank, the Heritage Foundation. Never mind that the event was initiated by Katherine Cave, founder of the non-partisan organization the Kelsey Coalition, or that Cave had been searching for speakers and a venue for *four years*. As Julia Beck, one of the panellists, said in an interview with Meghan Murphy for *Feminist Current*:

> Cave spent four years searching for anyone willing to speak publicly about how 'gender identity' impacts children and their

parents. She asked every left-leaning think tank she could find, but they either flatly refused with accusations of 'transphobia', or simply did not reply. Eventually, Cave and WoLF[2] worked together to plan a panel of left-leaning people to speak at the Heritage Foundation. . . . At the beginning of 2019, no other platform with half as much political influence as Heritage even dared to challenge the status quo, and that remains the case today.[3]

Beck's description suggests that the Heritage Foundation was a last-resort venue for women desperate to start a conversation about a topic they considered politically urgent. The backlash against those women suggests it would have been better for them to not have the event at all if they could not find a left-wing venue to host it.

Here's a more recent example – or, really, pair of examples – from my own patch of the forest. On 24 March 2024, a woman named Sabrinna Valisce declared on X (formerly Twitter) that 'Radical feminism is anti-Nazi, anti-neo-Nazi, anti-fascist & against totalitarianism & the far right. It is left wing & pro-choice. It stands for women & girls & the protection of children. We dont [sic] work with people who want the mass murder of Jews or the eugenics of homosexuals.'[4]

Setting aside the 'it is left wing and pro-choice' part for now, why would Valisce feel the need to make such an obvious statement? Valisce is a radical feminist, a position informed by her experience as a sex trade survivor,[5] and, most importantly for our purposes, an administrator for an online community of radical feminists from both Australia and New Zealand. A couple of days earlier, she had expelled the organizers of a Melbourne Women Will Speak rally from the online community, and posted to the group that:

Women's Action Group and [Women] Will Speak sadly must be banned from Aussie and Kiwi Radfems. Racism, Homophobia,

Nazism and neo-Nazi ideology is wholly incompatible with both Radical Feminism and any branch of Women's Rights. Admin has been sent video footage and photo's [sic] of a known neo-Nazi attending as an invited helper of the event this Saturday. We will NOT be endorsing or quietly capitulating to this tie with us. We reject these ties in their entirety and without hesitation.[6]

This storm in a very tiny teacup was just the latest in a string of skirmishes over who feminists should work with, centring in particular on alleged links to neo-Nazis. The year before, in the same month, the rather larger storm over the counter-protest by members of the National Socialist Network (a white supremacist group)[7] to a protest by socialists and trans activists of a Let Women Speak rally led to the expulsion of Victorian MP Moira Deeming from the parliamentary party room of the Liberal Party.[8] The problem, apparently, was the fact that Deeming co-hosted the rally, itself a feminist free speech event, with a British feminist accused of having associations with the far right.[9] (These 'associations' included, for example, appearing together in a photograph.) The fallout over the event resulted in three separate defamation lawsuits by feminist women, including Deeming, against the leader of the Victorian Liberal Party, John Pesutto.[10] In the 2024 iteration, the organizers of a Women Will Speak rally had been caught off guard by the size and noise of the protest against their event, and they made the decision to accept the offer of a better speaker from a man who had come to support the rally.[11] In return, he had asked to open and close the rally – although he made only brief, generic comments.[12] Soon after the event, he was alleged to be a neo-Nazi, and the women attending the rally and associated with its movement were, for the second year in a row, defending themselves from angry accusations of 'working with fascists'.[13]

One final example. In June 2024, as I was writing this Preface, a black British woman was being dogpiled on X for sharing a photo of herself wearing a British flag and tweeting 'you can [be] brown and still support your country'.[14] She had attended a protest against two-tier policing, but because the organizer of the protests was Tommy Robinson – a controversial figure in the United Kingdom known for opposition to immigration – opponents had apparently decided that expressions of patriotism by attendees were *really* white nationalism. (The woman then posted about the vitriol she had received and said that she was leaving the feminist movement as a result.)[15]

While 'working with' was stretched to conceptual implausibility in meaning 'standing in geographical proximity to' at the 2023 Let Women Speak rally, perhaps there *is* an understanding of 'working with' as 'sharing a platform with' that can be invoked for the 2024 Women Will Speak event, even though that is not what is normally meant when we talk about groups working together politically. Helen Joyce mentioned this understanding in a debate with Julie Bindel in 2022, provocatively titled 'Should TERFs Unite with the Right?', asking whether 'unite' was meant to mean working together, sharing a platform or something else – and whether these things were meant to be equally objectionable.[16]

The general claim that tends to be made during these flare-ups is that *feminists should not work with the right* (ally with the right, get in bed with the right, etc.). That the left owns minority groups – in the sense that the left, exclusively, champions the interests of minorities and is for that reason owed the allegiance of minorities – appears to be an unquestioned assumption of our current political life. This, in turn, gives rise to the sense of dissonance created by individuals who are both members of minority groups *and* have right-wing views: the black social conservative; the gay ultra-nationalist; the female libertarian; the impoverished enthusiast for capitalism. This same dissonance exists for women and feminism, creating a default assumption that a feminist is a left-wing woman. We

Preface   xi

don't make a distinction between *left-wing feminists* and feminists; it is assumed that we don't need to.

Do we need to, though? The claim that *feminists should not work with the right* is my target in this book. In the course of assessing this apparently narrow claim, we are taken to bigger questions about what it actually means to do feminist politics and the relation of feminism to the left-right political spectrum. To assess the plausibility of the claim that feminists should not work with the right, we'll need to talk about who *feminists* are, what *the left* and *the right* are, what reasons there are for why we shouldn't work with others, what reasons women have actually given (if any) for not working with the right, and what a feminism outside of the constraints of the political spectrum might look like – and whether *that* feminism would be preferable to a feminism exclusive to the left.

Let's get on with it.

1

Who Is a Feminist?

There are a lot of moving parts in the claim *feminists should not work with the right,* including *feminists, working with* and *the right.* We can't tackle them all at once, so let's focus on the *feminists* part of the claim for now, and then move on to the other parts in later chapters. To make a start on the claim that feminists should not work with the right, there is no getting around first figuring out who feminists *are.* If there can be 'white nationalist feminists', for example, then there can be no sense to the claim that feminists shouldn't work with white nationalists. (Some) feminists would *be* white nationalists, not merely others deciding whether to work *with* white nationalists. Let me make this point about who feminists are, and how this challenges our assumptions about the question of who feminists should work with, using the historical example of the conservative attorney and activist Phyllis Schlafly.[1]

Mainstream feminists in the United States in the 1970s were all campaigning hard for the ERA (Equal Rights Amendment), which declared that 'equality of rights under the law shall not be denied or abridged ... on account of sex', and gave the power to enforce this to Congress. Schlafly argued that equality of rights under the law is not in women's interests because

2 Who Is a Feminist?

there are specific protections – to her mind, privileges – that women had at the time that they should want to retain, not least exemption from the military draft and cheaper car insurance. She famously wrote, 'Why should we lower ourselves to "equal rights" when we already have the status of special privilege?"[2]

Schlafly's biographer, Carol Felsenthal, opens the chapter 'The Sweetheart of the Silent Majority' (in her book of the same name) with the following paragraph: 'For the ERA battle, Phyllis Schlafly forged a coalition that most political strategists would have considered a contradiction in terms – a coalition of Catholics, Fundamentalists, and Orthodox Jews. In this improbable alliance, party affiliation was a moot point, as was the ancient suspicion between Catholics and Fundamentalists, not to mention Jews and Fundamentalists.'[3]

Here we have a surprising coalition *within the right*, brought together on an issue Schlafly saw as being in women's interests, whose advisability we can ask about. Should the Catholics, or the Jews, have been prepared to work with the Fundamentalists? Is this good politics, setting aside differences in order to secure a common goal; or bad politics, sacrificing integrity to work with people you fundamentally disagree with, and in a way that might advance one of their aims to the detriment of other of your own? Is there a salient difference between asking whether Jews should work with Fundamentalists, and asking whether communists should work with anarchists, or radical feminists should work with intersectional feminists?

This takes us back to Valisce's claim, quoted in the Preface, that 'Radical feminism is . . . left wing and pro-choice'. Radical feminism *came out of* the left, but I do not see it as having any necessary connection, ideologically, to the left (more on this in chapters 2 and 3). And for feminism more generally, whether it is left wing surely depends on which kind of feminism we're talking about. Liberal feminism cannot be credibly described as left wing; most of the disagreements between left and right,

Who Is a Feminist? 3

at least within liberal democracies, are disagreements under the umbrella of liberalism, not outside of it.[4] Or in other words: liberal feminism is feminism within liberalism, which contains the left and the right. Socialist feminism probably can be described as left wing; most religious feminism probably can't.[5]

Of course, there is an open debate about the definition of 'feminist' and who counts as one. (There are also people who clearly count and yet refuse the label, usually because they repudiate the views of those most closely associated with it. But let's set that matter aside here and assume that being a feminist is a matter of satisfying the definition of feminist, not a matter of accepting the label of feminist.) I'll dismiss out of hand any definition which sets a pathetically low bar and makes it too easy for people to pay lip service to the idea of feminism without showing any real commitment. That means I won't consider views requiring only statements of belief, for example, the statement of a belief in the moral equality of the sexes. Instead, I'll consider definitions that require people to undertake *work* of a certain kind.[6] Consider the following:

1 A feminist is a [person] who works for women's equality.
2 A feminist is a [person] who works for women's self-determination.
3 A feminist is a [person] who works for women's liberation.
4 A feminist is a [person] who works against male dominance.
5 A feminist is 'a person who believes in and stands up for the political, economic and social equality of human beings'.[7]
6 A feminist is a [person] who works in women's interests as [the person] understands them.
7 A feminist is a [person] who works in women's interests as they really are.[8]

What kind of 'work'? It might be community organizing, volunteering, political campaigning, donating money, making in-kind contributions of resources or expertise to particular

Who Is a Feminist?

projects, showing up to events and protests, creating art, doing research, writing letters to the editor or phoning in to radio shows, and more. It might be taking on social costs (including social risks) to stand up for women when men, or other women, are putting them down. It might be women violating the norms and expectations of femininity. These actions need not be thought of or intended as feminist by the people who do them – individual women acting as social proof that a woman *can* do this kind of job or excel in this kind of sport or master this kind of craft all *do work* for women. (As Jessa Crispin has pointed out, Bjork has denied that she is a feminist, and yet she has moved the needle on ideas about what women can do and indeed has supported other women to do it.)[9]

Some of these definitions need refinement. Reference to 'equality' can contain a lot of ambiguity. Do we mean equality of outcome or equality of opportunity? What's the metric of equality, the thing that we ensure that men and women have equality *of*? Is it material goods, like money and assets, psychological goods like fulfilment and well-being, physical goods like health, or all of the above? This refinement matters because equality of outcome is more commonly associated with the left, while equality of opportunity is more commonly associated with the right, so *if* a feminist is (only) a person who works for women's equality, meaning women's equality of outcome with men, then it becomes correspondingly more plausible that feminism is an exclusively left-wing project.

Reference to 'women's self-determination' invites the question: *individual* self-determination or *collective* self-determination? If it is collective self-determination, then it is for the group, women, to decide together what it means to be a woman, what a good life for women looks like, and so on. If it is individual self-determination, then this is a matter for each individual to decide, and the feminist project may simply amount to making sure she's in the appropriate conditions (not distorting of her choices) to make that decision.

Who Is a Feminist?

Finally, reference to 'male domination' may be considered inadequate if we distinguish male *domination* from male *centredness* and male *identification*.[10] Male identification means that the things coded as 'for men' (male-typical, masculine) are more highly valued, so that people of both sexes tend to identify with or aspire to those things rather than the things coded as 'for women' (female-typical, feminine). Male centredness means certain practices or products take men as the template or standard – like thinking of 'sex' (in the sense of sexual intercourse) as something that starts with the penetration of a vagina by a penis and ends with the male orgasm, or like smartphones being a perfect fit for the average male's hand size (and not the average woman's).[11] These three thing may come apart in principle, and perhaps do come apart in some specific settings like workplaces. But they will often come together at the level of society – if men occupy most positions of power in Australian society, for example, it will be more likely that we'll also find Australian practices and products to be male centred, and Australians to be male identified in their attitudes. For that reason, I'll simply take all three together, using 'male dominance' as the shorthand for male dominance, male-centredness and male-identification.

Here's the list again, with the original Definitions 1 and 2 now separated into two versions each:

1. A feminist is a person who works for women's equality (of outcome).
2. A feminist is a person who works for women's equality (of opportunity).
3. A feminist is a person who works for women's collective self-determination.
4. A feminist is a person who works for women's individual self-determination.
5. A feminist is a person who works for women's liberation.
6. A feminist is a person who works against male dominance.

Who Is a Feminist?

7   A feminist is 'a person who believes in and stands up for the political, economic and social equality of human beings'.
8   A feminist is a person who works in women's interests as the person understands them.
9   A feminist is a person who works in women's interests as they really are.

Let's go through these, strike out any that are implausible and consider the rest as to whether they vindicate the idea that feminism is an exclusively left-wing project (that feminists should not work with the right).

I have argued elsewhere that self-determination is a crucial part of the project of feminism.[12] What I had in mind was the fact that, historically, women have been 'other determined', rather than self-determined, in particular, their lives have been largely determined by men. Men have owned women as property, controlled women through marriage, exploited women's labour, written books full of spurious claims about women's natures, frequently from a position of such authority that women have believed them. Men's ideas about women have shaped the cultures into which women are born. Self-determination is a response to this history: it is *women* who must decide, for themselves, what a woman is, and what it means to be a woman. Men have done enough damage! (This was also my reason for originally insisting that only a woman could be a feminist, and a man could be at best a feminist ally.)[13]

I continue to think there is something important in this view, but it has also been brought to my attention that thinking of feminism in terms of women's *collective* self-determination produces some undesirable results. First, what a woman *is* doesn't seem like a matter for a group to decide; it seems like a matter for which there is a scientific answer: a woman is an adult human female.[14] Second, what a woman *is like*, or what a good life for a woman looks like, doesn't seem like a

Who Is a Feminist?

matter that should be given over to majority decision. Suppose there was a conservative religious resurgence, and the majority of women decided that what a woman is like is *caring, warm and nurturing,* and what a good life for a woman looks like, distinct from a man, is *raising children and maintaining the home.* Should progressive non-religious women then be tied to this view of women because that is what women as a group have decided? My intuition is *no, they shouldn't.* We might take another example from the fact that some progressive women today have accepted the idea that 'woman' and 'man' are terms that refer to gender identities rather than sexes. Suppose a majority of women came on board with that view, that a woman is a person of either sex who identifies as a woman. Should other women be tied to that definition of 'woman' because that's what the majority believes? Again, the answer seems to be 'no'. We can incorporate the resistance to being other-determined (determined by men) by thinking of individual self-determination as taking place in conditions that *exclude* the influence of men who seek an understanding of women that serves men's interests. This might justify women-only consciousness-raising groups, for example, as important contexts in which feminists make decisions about how they want to determine their own individual lives. (But note that one does not have to *be* a woman to work *for* those conditions for women.) For these reasons, we should strike Definition 3 from the list.

1 A feminist is a person who works for women's equality (of outcome).
2 A feminist is a person who works for women's equality (of opportunity).
3 ~~A feminist is a person who works for women's collective self-determination.~~
4 A feminist is a person who works for women's individual self-determination.

8 Who Is a Feminist?

5 A feminist is a person who works for women's liberation.
6 A feminist is a person who works against male dominance.
7 A feminist is 'a person who believes in and stands up for the political, economic and social equality of human beings'.
8 A feminist is a person who works in women's interests as the person understands them.
9 A feminist is a person who works in women's interests as they really are.

Definition 7 comes from the @UN_Women X (previously Twitter) account in 2019. It does not deserve the name *feminism*, given as it is a definition of persons who believe in the equality of *human beings*. It's one thing to think that men can be feminists; it's another thing again to think that anyone who stands up for the equality of human beings *is a feminist*. If you're struggling to see this, just think of a man who is passionately opposed to feminism on the grounds that *men, not women, are oppressed* and dedicates his life to the fight against military conscription, which he takes to be the worst of the elements of men's oppression. On @UN_Women's definition, this man is a *feminist*. That is absurd. So Definition 7 should also be struck from the list.

1 A feminist is a person who works for women's equality (of outcome).
2 A feminist is a person who works for women's equality (of opportunity).
3 ~~A feminist is a person who works for women's collective self-determination.~~
4 A feminist is a person who works for women's individual self-determination.
5 A feminist is a person who works for women's liberation.
6 A feminist is a person who works against male dominance.
7 ~~A feminist is 'a person who believes in and stands up for the political, economic and social equality of human beings'.~~

Who Is a Feminist?

8 A feminist is a person who works in women's interests as the person understands them.
9 A feminist is a person who works in women's interests as they really are.

Definition 8 also throws up some challenges. Consider a Christian woman who endorses a complementary thesis: that God created man and woman differently and complementary to one another. On her view, it is *not* in women's interests that workplaces make paternity leave mandatory (in order to combat male stigma around taking parental leave and to counteract the disincentives to companies of hiring women employees of childbearing age and then having to pay out maternity leave only to them – which makes men appear the more attractive hires).[15] No law or policy that works for women's *sameness* with men will be in women's interests as this woman understands them because in her view women are different from men, and what is needed is for women's difference to be accommodated such that women can lead good lives qua *women*.[16] How the Christian woman we're thinking of fills out the details of what is in women's interests will be very different to how a feminist with a sameness standard fills out those details.[17] But say the 'work' she does is for the equal recognition of women's contributions as being on a par with men's – we need *both* family life and work, and the work of creating and sustaining family life is important and honourable. It is hard for me to see why this woman should not be considered a feminist just because other women reject complementarianism. (And I say this as someone who rejects complementarianism.)

Consider next a religion that contains as doctrine not just a complementarity thesis but also a clear hierarchy of man over woman, so that a woman who believes in this religion is committed not only to women's *difference from* men but also to women's *inferiority to* men.[18] There's something peculiar about insisting that a male-supremacist woman can be a feminist,

10   Who Is a Feminist?

just as it would be peculiar to insist that a white supremacist Black person is somehow still an anti-racist. We can go one of two ways at this point. The first is to take this to be a decisive objection to Definition 8. It permits a male supremacist to count as a feminist; it is obvious that male supremacists cannot be feminists; therefore, this is an inadequate definition of a feminist. Rather than countenancing as feminists people with *any* understanding at all of what is in women's interests, we should limit what that understanding can be, or use one of the other definitions not put in terms of women's interests. (Definition 9 has its own problems, in particular how we can know the objective truth about what is actually in women's interests.)

The other way to go is to accept the peculiarity of a male-supremacist feminist as a cost of keeping Definition 8 on the table. A moral/legal distinction may help to make this more palatable. Clearly, some things are morally desirable yet inappropriate subjects of legislation. It is very annoying when a friend is always late. But it would not be the right response to introduce a law allowing us to seek damages from our friends to compensate for our wasted time. So too we might think that a religious woman can be a male supremacist and yet think women's submission is an interpersonal matter; she may proselytize about the joys of hierarchical family life and yet not use the law to *force* hierarchical family life on all other women, whether they want it or not. If that's right, it limits the scope of the 'work' she can do in order to count as a feminist. Perhaps she works for divorce laws that protect a woman's ability to remain adequately accommodated and able to provide for her children in the event that her husband is unfaithful or abusive. In my view, the costs of accepting that there can be male-supremacist feminists are lower than the costs of stipulating that to count as a feminist one must accept a specific view of women's interests.[19] The latter would exclude many more people who are doing important work *for* women, and

Who Is a Feminist? 11

we already have the resources to deny that the woman we're thinking of is a *particular kind of* feminist. For example, if radical feminism is committed to the sameness of women and men, then radical feminists can repudiate the religious women just described as *radical* feminists. We can be generous about who counts as a feminist and strict about who counts as a specific type of feminist.[20]

With the initial list of definitions now refined, and two struck out, do any of the remaining definitions rule out the possibility of a right-wing feminism and thereby show that feminism is an exclusively left-wing project? The first, stated in terms of working for women's equality *of outcome* with men, takes men as the standard for equality. Women are equal *to men* when they have *what men have*. So anyone who rejects this measure cannot be a feminist on this definition. If *all* right-wing people reject this measure, then *no* right-wing person can be a feminist, leaving the path clear for the claim that feminism is an exclusively left-wing project. Conservatives who believe the sexes are complementary (or hierarchical) rather than equal will reject this measure, but not all conservatives believe the sexes are complementary (or hierarchical). Radical feminists who believe that men are not the measure of women's equality – and for this reason speak in terms of liberation rather than equality (using Definition 5 instead of Definitions 1 or 2) – as well as *any* person who thinks that there are some sex differences that make equality of opportunity a more appropriate goal than equality of outcome, will also reject this definition. There might be more people who reject the definition on the right than on the left because there are more religious people on the right than on the left. But we're looking for a definition that vindicates the claim that feminism is an exclusively left-wing project. Merely showing that *more* right-wing than left-wing people will fail to count as feminists according to a particular definition is not a vindication of that claim. So

12 Who Is a Feminist?

Definition 1 does not rule out the possibility of right-wing feminism.

People from anywhere on the political spectrum could both believe in, and work against, male dominance (Definition 6); and could be committed to, and work for, women's equality of opportunity with men (Definition 2); women's individual self-determination (Definition 4); women's liberation (Definition 5); and/or women's interests (as they understand them, and if they get lucky, as they really are) (Definitions 8 and 9). It might be that people from different religions, cultures, educational backgrounds, economic classes, political party affiliations and political ideologies have different beliefs about what is wrong (if anything) between the sexes in the current social context, but so long as some of them think that *something* is wrong, there's room on most of these definitions for any such people to be feminists. Schlafly was very clearly working in women's interests as she understood them, so on that definition at least she was a feminist. (Many people will find this claim surprising, given that Schlafly is frequently described as an anti-feminist, given her opposition to the mainstream feminists of the time.)[21]

The definition that would seem to get closest to vindicating thinking of feminism as an exclusively left-wing project is Definition 7, the one offered by @UN_Women – at least if we think of equality for all in terms of equality of outcome. But we have already struck it off, for the reason that it permits thinking of a person whose work has nothing to do with women as a feminist.

David Benatar, in his book *The Second Sexism*, distinguishes 'egalitarian feminists' from 'partisan feminists' and, while he uses the word 'feminists' for both, it is clear that he thinks egalitarian feminism is the legitimate project of the two. As he sees it, this is 'the distinction between those feminists who are motivated by and interested in equality of the sexes and those feminists whose primary concern is the advancement of women and girls'.[22] An egalitarian feminist is ultimately motivated by equality. Because she sees women being wrongfully discriminated against in comparison to men, she works *against* that discrimination. But if someone were to bring other inequalities to her attention, she would need to – on pain of inconsistency – care about those too.[23] (That is what *The Second Sexism* does: attempts to bring to her – and others' – attention wrongful discrimination against men.) On this way of thinking about equality, men are not the standard for equality of outcome against which women are measured. Rather, in some – but importantly, not all – of the cases where men and women are treated differently, *men* are wrongfully discriminated against when they do not have what women have, and *women* are wrongfully discriminated against when they do not have what men have. Either sex can count as wrongfully discriminated against, and either sex can be the standard of equality for the other. This is not an objection to Definition 1 as I have stated it because Benatar does not think that feminists must *work for* men's equality, only that they should care about it and not get in the way of those who are working for it.[24]

A 'partisan feminist', on Benatar's account, is 'the equivalent of those men's rights advocates who are interested only in advancing the interests and protecting the rights of males'.[25] In drawing a parallel to men's rights advocates, Benatar positions 'partisan feminism' as a special interest group for women, functioning as a union or lobby group might do. He cites as one example the second-wave radical feminist group New York Radical Women, who declared, 'We take the woman's side in everything. We ask not if something is "reformist", "radical", "revolutionary" or "moral". We ask: is it good for women or bad for women?'[26] It's significant, however, that New York Radical Women were writing at the start of the second wave in a context in which women were not yet considered a class/caste, and *no one* took the woman's side in everything. Taking

14   Who Is a Feminist?

women's side was a political act. I doubt that Benatar would go back to the start of anti-racist activism and declare its thinkers and activists 'partisan anti-racists' because they didn't pay enough attention to white people's problems. But setting that aside, does his distinction between 'egalitarian feminism' and 'partisan feminism' divide the definitions on our list, cast the partisan definitions as illegitimate, and help to show that feminism is exclusively left wing after all?

It does divide the list. Definitions 1 and 2 invoke equality in a way that is compatible with assuming that feminists have a background commitment to equality and have simply chosen to work on women's inequality with men. Definitions 4, 5, 6, 8 and 9 invoke self-determination, liberation, (opposition to) domination and interests. All of these might well be partisan, or at least need not be egalitarian (although presumably there is some explanation for *why* a woman has chosen to work on these things, and that will usually be because she thinks women lack them). But feminists need not have a background commitment to equality that generates their more specific motivation to work on women's issues. They may simply have a direct interest in women's issues. It may be that once women's issues are resolved, they would cease to have any interest in social justice projects or in politics. There are a million reasons for why people choose to work on particular projects. This is a challenge to the very distinction Benatar makes, which appears to assume feminists need some grand justification for working on women's issues, one which they can be held to as a way of generating reasons for them to care about other things.

Furthermore, a feminist might think that men's long history of domination makes them unfit to be taken as the measure of equality for women, even if we accept Benatar's claim that there are some cases in which women can be taken as the measure of equality for men. Perhaps there is a universal standard of equality – what any human should have – that is entirely different from what either women or men have now, and we won't know what it consists in until we achieve a world without sex hierarchy. What women should have is something else entirely *because* what both men and women should have is something else entirely. Similarly, a feminist might think that men and women are different in ways that are relevant to their flourishing, so that the realization of women's self-determination, the achievement of women's liberation and the satisfaction of women's interests all require something different than men's self-determination, interests and/or liberation would. So Definitions 4, 5, 6, 8 and 9 don't commit us to thinking of a feminist as a kind of union representative for women (or feminism as a union for women), who would push for women's advantage in the workplace long after they were the most advantaged people there. This is not to say there are no 'partisan feminists' in Benatar's terms; it is to say that a partisan feminist isn't necessarily what he thinks it is, and in my view is not remotely illegitimate. Feminists take the woman's side because the woman's side needs taking, and most men sure aren't taking it.[27] Because we have not found sufficient reason to reject the 'partisan' definitions, we do not need to move to the next stage of working out whether egalitarian feminism is left-wing-only feminism.

In my view, all the remaining definitions are adequate, and disagreement over the exact goal of feminism – e.g., women's *equality* or women's *liberation*? – is reasonable among feminists rather than unreasonable between those who are feminists and those who are not. Thus we can roll them together into a single flexible definition:

> *Feminist*: a person who works for women's equality (whether of outcome or of opportunity), women's individual self-determination, women's liberation or women's interests (as the person understands them, whether or not that is also as they are); or who works against male dominance.[28]

16   Who Is a Feminist?

Just as none of the remaining definitions alone ruled out a right-wing feminism, neither does this single flexible definition, which simply combines them.

The idea that feminism is an exclusively left-wing project probably owes its credibility to the idea that what justifies feminism is a more general opposition to social hierarchy; oppression in any form; the moral equality of persons. *Because* women are subordinated in a social hierarchy along the axis of sex, or women are oppressed on the basis of sex, or women are not yet equal to men, feminism is needed. If this is right, then what @UN_Women were getting wrong is foregrounding the background assumption. Commitment to equality for all isn't feminism; but feminism is one part of the project of achieving equality for all – so for anyone who has that project, *they* will also be feminists. One way that some people draw the distinction between the left and the right is in terms of an opposition to social hierarchy and oppression, and a commitment to equality, so that is one way to make sense of the idea that feminism is a left-wing project.[29]

But the strength of this view depends on whether that is a credible way to draw the distinction between the left and the right. Many people on the right would deny that they are *for* social hierarchy, oppression or inequality and say that this is just the simplistic thinking of progressives who wish to carve the world up into heroes and villains, and unsurprisingly assign themselves to the heroes' side. As Helen Joyce memorably put it:

> I've been repeatedly told that it's impossible to be a feminist unless you are on the left. So that means that I'm not a feminist – and I've regarded myself as a feminist since I was a young girl. I think what happens here is that people on the left think that they're good and the people on the right are bad. And the really strange bit is they think that we all agree with them, including

the people on the right. So they think we're in Middle Earth, and that the left is the Hobbits and the Elves, and the right is Sauron and the Orcs. So we're in a world where there's good against evil and everybody knows who's good and who's evil.[30]

Going forward, I'll work on the assumption that people from anywhere on the political spectrum can be feminists, and that any of them might face questions about who to work with – or indeed, angry accusations that they're 'undermining the feminist movement' because of who they've chosen to work with.

While there's a default assumption *now* that feminism is a left-wing project, that hasn't always been the case. One of the most famous suffragettes founded a Women's Party with an explicitly right-wing political platform. Some of the 1960s radicals came to the view that feminism was impossible within the left. In the next chapter, we'll take a look at the radicals' reasons, and consider whether they're still relevant today in pushing back against the default association of feminism with the left. Then, in chapter 3, I'll turn to some of the more obvious tensions thrown up by the idea of a 'right-wing feminism'.

2

The 1960s:
Feminists Leaving the Left

> Women have left the movement in droves. The obvious reasons
> are that we are tired of being sex slaves and doing shitwork for
> men whose hypocrisy is so blatant in their political stance of
> liberation for everybody (else). But there is really a lot more to
> it than that. I can't quite articulate it yet.
>
> Carol Hanisch, 2006 [1969]

The women's liberation movement emerged in the United States in the late 1960s, and attempts to address the treatment of women by men within left-wing political movements began around 1965. Many women *left* the left in order to pursue women's liberation; the radical feminists were explicitly separatist. In a 1968 paper titled 'Toward a Female Liberation Movement', Beverly Jones and Judith Brown wrote of the male-dominated left, 'Our vision must not be limited by theirs. We must urge in speech and in print that women go their own way.'[1] Women going their own way might sound funny today, given the notoriety of MGTOW (Men Going Their Own Way).[2] But left-wing women in the late 1960s were frustrated by their place within leftist politics and what they saw as the refusal of leftist men to take women's issues seriously. This is an interesting historical

The 1960s: Feminists Leaving the Left 19

moment when it comes to the question of whether feminism is an exclusively left-wing project because it relates to types of feminism that emerged *from* the left and yet split from the left. If we can understand the reasons for the split, that might give us a clearer understanding of the relationship between feminism and the left. The earliest four magazines of the women's liberation movement, all with issues published in 1968, were *Lilith, No More Fun and Games, Notes from the First Year* and *Voice of the WLM.* So let's have a look at some of the essays addressing this matter of the split.

A memo, 'Sex and Caste', was initially circulated privately late in 1965 and printed early the following year in the New Left's *Liberation Magazine.* The memo, written by Casey Hayden and Mary King, noted that 'there seem to be many parallels that can be drawn between treatment of Negroes and treatment of women in our society as a whole', and that

> Many people who are very hip to the implications of the racial caste system, even people in the movement, don't seem to be able to see the sexual caste system, and if the question is raised they respond with: 'That's the way it's supposed to be. There are biological differences.' Or with other statements which recall a white segregationist confronted with integration.[3]

They noted the way that sex roles applied inside their political movement, 'ranging from relationships of women organizers to men in the community, to who cleans the freedom house, to who holds leadership positions, to who does secretarial work, and who acts as spokesman for groups'.[4] It's striking how little hope Hayden and King appeared to hold out for the possibility of feminism at that time (even more striking, considering that Betty Friedan's *The Feminine Mystique* had been published two years earlier and become a bestseller): 'Objectively, the chances seem nil that we could get a movement based on anything as distant to American thought as a sex-caste system. Therefore, most of us will probably want to work full-time on problems such as war, poverty, race.'[5] They were arguing to open up some space in the movement for discussions about 'all the problems between men and women and all the problems of women functioning in society as equal human beings'[6] precisely because there was no other space for those discussions.

In an essay about Casey Hayden's contributions at the origins of all three of the Student Non-Violent Coordinating Committee (SNCC), Students for a Democratic Society (SDS) and the Women's Liberation Movement, the historian Harold L. Smith emphasizes an increasing awareness among women in the SNCC and SDS of male members' attitudes towards women.[7] Hayden[8] had been involved in desegregation actions in Austin, Texas, nearly a full year before the North Carolina 'sit-ins that are credited with starting the 1960s civil rights movement'.[9] She was the person who convinced the National Student Association in 1960 to endorse desegregation sit-ins.[10] And yet, when working in SDS's national office in the summer of 1961, 'she spent the summer ... typing [SDS's] entire mailing list onto stencils while the men discussed strategy'.[11] On New Year's Eve, with a party planned, 'the men continued their discussion while the women went upstairs and set up food and drink'.[12] Hayden studied English and philosophy, and outside of university undertook 'serious study' of the work of Camus[13]; her university education surely informed her judgement that 'SDS meetings usually involved intense discussions that too often seemed to Casey like intellectual posturing by young males'.[14] Smith quotes from Hayden's ex-husband's memoir that she once left such a meeting declaring, 'I seriously believe y'all are discussing bullshit.'[15] In SDS meetings, 'men often ignored women's comments ... as if small children had spoken during a discussion among adults'.[16] Hayden herself had enough experience and authority to not be treated this

The 1960s: Feminists Leaving the Left   21

way, but Smith writes that 'she empathized with the women who were'.[17]

In considering the reasons historically offered for feminists to split from the left, we can extract three from Hayden's experiences:

- Leftist men naturalize women's 'difference' from men and so do not see it as an injustice, so feminists must leave the left.
- The distribution of labour within the leftist movement is sexist (and unlikely to change), so feminists must leave the left.
- Women's contributions to theory and strategy are ignored or dismissed by leftist men, so feminists must leave the left.

Ellen Willis, one of the founders of the radical feminist group Redstockings, wrote in a 1968 *Guardian* article 'Women and the Left'[18] about a political rally[19] in January 1968 that included a women's liberation presentation. Not only was the issue of women's liberation left out of the *Guardian*'s ad for the rally, left off the photocopies of the programme and not mentioned in the announcement at the start of the rally, 'Mobe[20] spokesman Dave Dellinger announced at the Saturday rally that the Mobe had come to demonstrate against the war and for black liberation. When some women on the stage yelled at him, he mentioned women's liberation as an afterthought' – but during the women's presentation 'men in the audience booed, laughed, catcalled, and yelled enlightened remarks like "Take her off the stage and fuck her"'.[21]

This gives us a fourth reason for feminists to split from the left:

- Leftist men sexualize and degrade women, so feminists must leave the left.

A July 1967 issue of *New Left Notes*, the magazine of SDS, included an article produced by the Women's Liberation Workshop, imploring the men of SDS to support the women's liberation project. It was accompanied by a rather unfortunate image of a woman dressed like a small child in a polka-dot babydoll dress with bloomers showing, holding a large sign reading 'We want our Rights & We want them NOW!' The authors demanded of their 'brothers' that they 'recognize that they must deal with their own problems of male chauvinism in their personal, social and political relationships', and said, 'We recognize the difficulty our brothers will have in dealing with male chauvinism and we will assume our full responsibility in helping to resolve the contradiction.'[22] They also stated more general demands for men to share in childcare and housework; for birth control and abortion access; and for women's full inclusion 'in all aspects of movement work'.[23]

That article was ridiculed by Jones in her part of the article written together with Judith Brown that was mentioned at the start of this chapter. Jones called it 'ludicrous', 'pathetic' and 'fantastic' (in the pejorative sense), comparing it with 'all the fruitless approaches black groups made and are still making to local white power groups'.[24] Jones argued that 'radical females' – meaning females involved with SDS – failed to 'understand the desperate condition of women in general', likely in virtue of occupying a 'sexy, sexless, limbo' as students, before becoming wives and/or mothers. She argued, 'For their own salvation and for the good of the movement, women must form their own group and work primarily for female liberation.'[25] It is worth quoting more fully her comment about exoduses from 'the movement':

> One of the best things that ever happened to black militants happened when they got hounded out of the stars-and-stripes, white-controlled civil rights movement, when they started fighting for blacks instead of the American Dream. The best

The 1960s: Feminists Leaving the Left   23

thing that ever happened to potential white radicals in civil rights happened when they got thrown out by SNCC and were forced to face their own oppression in their own world. When they started fighting for control of the universities, against the draft, the war, and the business order. And the best thing that may yet happen to potentially radical young women is that they will be driven out of both of these groups. That they will be forced to stop fighting for the 'movement' and start fighting primarily for the liberation and independence of women.[26]

Jones is here anticipating the Combahee River Collective that is now better known for this sentiment, which has come to be known as 'identity politics'. It would write 11 years later that 'the only people who care enough about us to work consistently for our liberation is us', and 'the most profound and potentially the most radical politics come directly out of our own identity, as opposed to working to end somebody else's oppression'.[27] The New Left projects, like opposition to the Vietnam War, were 'somebody else's oppression', while women's liberation was for women 'our own identity'. Jones maintained that

[o]nly when they [women] seriously undertake this struggle will they begin to understand that they aren't just ignored or exploited – they are feared, despised, and enslaved . . . no sweet-talking list of grievances and demands, no appeal to male conscience, no behind-the-scenes or in-the-home maneuvering [sic] is going to get power for women. If they want freedom, equality, and respect, they are going to have to organize and fight for them realistically and radically.[28]

After a lengthy tirade against the domestic position of women, Jones finishes her part of the article by describing some of the 'projects I think women my age must undertake as part of the overall movement'.[29] Here, she does not mean the

24   The 1960s: Feminists Leaving the Left

left but the *feminist* movement: 'Let's get together to decide in groups of women how to get out of this bind, to discover and fight the techniques of domination in and out of the home. To change our physical and social surroundings to free our time, our energy, and our minds – to start to build for ourselves, for all mankind, a world without horrors.'[30]

She defended, in particular, women focusing on their own issues. As she put it (here, somewhat confusingly, the reference of 'movement' having shifted back to the left): 'Women must resist pressure to enter into movement activities other than their own. There cannot be real restructuring of this society until the relationships between the sexes are restructured.'[31] Women must stop rewarding men who 'commit any horror' or 'suffer any mutilation of their souls' in public life with 'awe, respect, and perhaps love' when they return to the home. This is where she insists, as noted already above, that 'Our vision must not be limited by theirs. We must urge in speech and in print that women go their own way.'[32]

Jones included among the feminist projects self-defence classes for women, forcing the media to portray women positively and accurately, women sharing their experiences under patriarchy with each other, communities built to ease women's 'double-shift' (e.g., housing built around schools with cafeterias, extracurricular activities for children and babysitting services), women learning their history, women investigating sex differences, women defending equal pay for equal work, women fighting against discrimination in college admissions and in hiring, and a guaranteed income; and, finally, legal and available contraception and abortion.[33]

This gives us a fifth and sixth reason:

- Feminism should be practised as identity politics; the left is not identity politics for women (it is not women fighting against 'their own' oppression), so feminists must leave the left.[34]

- If women remain in the left, they will reward leftist men with 'awe, respect, and . . . love', and this will prevent the restructuring of the relationship between the sexes, so feminists must leave the left.

The first issue of the women's liberation magazine *No More Fun and Games* includes Roxanne Dunbar's essay 'Slavery' and Maureen Davidica's essay 'Women and the Radical movement'. Dunbar wrote about women being asked to wait until 'after the revolution' – to prioritize other causes and wait their turn.[35] Her response was 'we must say No, just as the Black man has said No, we shall not wait and serve in the meantime. The situation is too serious.'[36] Alice Echols describes the radical feminists of New York Radical Women as being clear on this same point: 'All three women'– Rosalyn Baxandall, Carol Hanisch and Ellen Willis – 'maintain that they made a distinction between an individual woman's participation in the left – which they believed was valid, at the very least – and the attachment of women's liberation to the left – which, they argued, resulted in its subordination to the left.'[37]

Davidica was even clearer: 'This is a call for separatism, for radical women to dissociate themselves from male-oriented, male-dominated radical organizations and join together in Women's Liberation groups as the most effective way to achieve their own independent identity and the liberation of all women.'[38] In her view, it was not only that the radical projects of the time – 'people dying from American imperialist oppression in Vietnam, in the ghettoes, in the California grape fields, etc. . . . the black liberation movement'[39] – were taken to have 'prior importance' over women's liberation, but that those projects actually worked *against* women's liberation. She says that the 'underground radical society' in fact depends on the continued exploitation of women:

26   The 1960s: Feminists Leaving the Left

> Women's liberation has not come about in the underground radical society because it is also against the interests of that society which still uses the traditional definitions of masculine/feminine to perpetuate the role of woman as inferior – so she will be content doing the shitwork for the organization, not even attempting policy discussion; content to loyally sit in the background at steering committee meetings while the men hash out the direction of the revolution; content to follow that direction in demonstrations and in the streets (like soldiers following officers' orders in any traditional military situation), and finally, content in her traditional supportive role as comforter for the radical male exhausted from the competition and energy consuming rat race of radical politics.[40]

She goes on to write, 'Radical politics is a man's business because politics is traditionally a man's business; the draft is all male, the war is all male, the power structures of both system and radical politics are all male (with a few token females).'[41] On this view, it was *no accident* that the left cared about racism but not about sexism: racism affected men. A similar thought is echoed in another essay of Dunbar's in the same issue of the magazine: 'We shall not fight on the enemy's grounds – on his streets, in his courts, legislatures, "radical" movements, marriage, media.'[42]

A little later in the essay, there is a different criticism, this one to do with the *effectiveness* of the left: 'The "radical" groups in this society and probably in all the "rich" states are masturbatory and ineffective.'[43] This could just mean that they happen to be made up of men who are more interested in self-congratulation than outcomes. But it could also mean *that is just what 'radical' is*, men getting together to pretend to be revolutionaries. Then feminists' reasons not to work with the left would be the posturing and inefficacy of leftists.

This gives us four more reasons for feminists to leave the left:

The 1960s: Feminists Leaving the Left   27

- The left asks women to wait until 'after the revolution'; women's issues are too urgent to be postponed; so feminists must leave the left.
- Radical politics, just like every other major institution, is male dominated; feminists must fight *against*, not *together with*, what is male dominated; so feminists must leave the left.
- The 'underground radical society' of the left depends on the exploitation of women; feminism is a movement against women's exploitation; so feminists must leave the left.
- 'Radicals' are just men getting together to pretend to be revolutionaries; feminists want to be actual revolutionaries; so feminists must leave the left (cease to be 'radicals').

Marlene Dixon, writing in her essay 'On Women's Liberation' in 1970, makes a different point, one about working with leftist *women*.[44] Where the complaint about leftist men was their sexism and their refusal to take the women's liberation issue seriously, Dixon's complaint about leftist women was the extent to which they were beholden to the 'invisible audience' of movement (leftist) men, and movement (leftist) theory.[45] She wrote of the first national women's liberation conference in 1968 that

> [m]uch of the pathology of the conference, particularly in terms of personal animosity and suspicion, could be directly traced to the degree to which each woman was still dependent upon men for her evaluation of herself. The boldest and most fearless women were clearly those who had bolted from, or never belonged to, established leftist organizations; they were followed by those women still in such organizations, but active in women's auxiliaries.[46]

Her diagnosis was that 'the real split among the women hinged upon the significant audience that women addressed: other

28 The 1960s: Feminists Leaving the Left

women, or Movement men'.[47] Those women who had left, or never belonged to, the left stood for 'militance on behalf of women' and for 'independent women and women's liberation as first priority'.[48] They also had 'complete contempt' for those women whose primary audience was leftist men.[49] These women 'dismissed the leftists as unliberated spokeswomen for the submersion of the women's struggle in the "revolutionary struggle"'.[50]

A vivid example of this 'split' comes from the example Dixon gives of the United Front Against Fascism conference run by the Black Panther Party. There was to be a women's panel on the first evening of the conference, but the conference started late and a rumour circulated that the panel was to be cancelled. During one of the opening speeches, 'a large number of women stood up to protest silently the cancellation of the women's panel'. The women's panel was *not* cancelled in the end; and Dixon writes that it was unclear whether the Panthers understood that the silent protest related to the women's panel or was instead taken to be general disruption (the fact that they denounced it as the work of 'pig-provocateurs' suggests the latter).[51] What is significant is what happened the next day: 'a group of women, identified with various leftist sects, came to defend the Panthers.'[52] They attacked the protesting women as 'counter-revolutionary lackeys of Capitalism, objectively racist, etc.'[53] As Dixon points out, the women they were attacking 'were long-term supporters of the Panthers and were some of the best radical women in the country'.[54] The independent women were simply pushing for the women's panel to go ahead – for women's liberation to be a part of the discussion within the radical project of Black liberation. Leftist women showed up to 'defend' the Black liberation movement by attacking the women's liberationists as 'racist', 'capitalist', and so on. Dixon writes:

> The sectarian women apparently had approached the meeting with a stereotype so grotesque, and so typically male, that com-

The 1960s: Feminists Leaving the Left   29

munication was impossible. Charges of being 'petty bourgeois', 'men-haters', 'objectively racist', and so on, contained all of the men's invective against the women's movement. The non-sectarian women reacted defensively, over-reacted in fact, to their attackers. There was little if any truth in the accusations, but the women were pushed almost to a frenzy by the fact that other women were using the men's line to attack them.[55]

This is not just an issue about the 'invisible audience' (other women or leftist men), but also about women's priorities. Leftist women prioritized the left, and so would attack women's liberationists for being insufficiently anti-capitalist.[56] There was a serious disagreement among women over which causes deserved their attention and ought to be prioritized. There was also a problem of opportunism, with leftist women *using* women's liberation meetings as opportunities to recruit women to leftist causes.[57]

Alice Echols describes this rift in her book *Daring to Be Bad*, using the terminology of 'feminists' and 'politicos'. Feminists were women who prioritized women; politicos were women who prioritized the left. While there were rifts over other issues, like leadership and marriage, Echols reports that the big rift was that between feminists and politicos.[58] (Socialist feminism emerged as a kind of compromise, aimed at 'organizing women simultaneously around the issues of gender and class' – although as Echols notes, class often ended up 'the dominant partner in this marriage'.[59]) In a 1970 talk given at the University of Rhode Island, Ti-Grace Atkinson noted that this rift has a longer history: even during the first wave of feminism (whose predominant concern was suffrage), there was the National Woman Suffrage Association, 'those women who placed women first at all times', and the American Woman Suffrage Association, 'those women who did not always put women foremost'.[60] Only in 1890, 'when there were no longer any other distracting political issues such as slavery, the vote

30   The 1960s: Feminists Leaving the Left

for black men, or a war involving this country [the United States] in any major way' did the two associations join forces.[61] While the National Organization of Women (N.O.W.) was considered on the 'politicos' side and women's liberation was considered on the 'feminists' side, Atkinson described the difference between the two as residing in 'the politics of the men to whom these women were attached'.[62]

I finish our list with two final reasons:

- Radical *women* are beholden to an 'invisible audience' of leftist men; the 'boldest and most fearless' women's liberationists were those who had fled or never belonged to leftist organizations. Feminists must leave the left – not just because of leftist men but also because of leftist women.
- Leftists prioritize the left: they have attacked feminists for being insufficiently anti-capitalist; they have used women's liberation meetings as left-recruitment opportunities. Feminists prioritize women. This is an irreconcilable conflict in priorities, so feminists must leave the left.

So we have our reasons all in one place. Here is the full list of reasons given in this period for why feminists must leave the left:

- Leftist men naturalize women's 'difference' from men and so do not see it as an injustice.
- The distribution of labour within the leftist movement is sexist.
- Women's contributions to theory and strategy are ignored or dismissed by leftist men.
- Leftist men sexualize and degrade women.
- Feminism should be practised as identity politics; the left is not identity politics for women (it is not women fighting against 'their own' oppression).

The 1960s: Feminists Leaving the Left   31

- If women remain in the left, they will reward leftist men with 'awe, respect, and ... love' and this will prevent the restructuring of the relationship between the sexes.
- The left asks women to wait until 'after the revolution'; women's issues are too urgent to be postponed.
- Radical politics, just like every other major institution, is male dominated; feminists must fight *against*, not *together with*, what is male dominated.
- The 'underground radical society' of the left depends on the exploitation of women; feminism is a movement against women's exploitation.
- 'Radicals' are just men getting together to pretend to be revolutionaries; feminists want to be actual revolutionaries.
- Radical *women* are beholden to an 'invisible audience' of leftist men, the 'boldest and most fearless' women's liberationists were those who had fled or never belonged to leftist organizations.
- Leftists prioritize the left: they have attacked feminists for being insufficiently anti-capitalist; they have used women's liberation meetings as left-recruitment opportunities. Feminists prioritize women. This is an irreconcilable conflict in priorities.

Notice that at least some of what is being expressed here is a problem with *leftist men* (or, perhaps, men), not a problem with the left, ideologically speaking. Of course, if you think that 'the left' is only ever the people who profess to be 'of the left' (on which more in chapter 4), then this will be a meaningless distinction. The men at the time were the left, and the men at the time were sexist; therefore the left at the time was sexist. That was a good reason for women to leave the left. (Whether that means they go to the right, or go nowhere, is a separate question, and one which radical and gender-critical feminist women today are also grappling with.) But if 'the left' is more than those who profess to be 'of the left', if it is a

32 The 1960s: Feminists Leaving the Left

political ideology or a set of commitments that people, sexist and otherwise, can sign up to and yet fall short of (perhaps far short), then leftist men's sexism may have been a reason for women to leave *leftist men*, without yet being a reason to leave *the left*. Just consider, for example, if it turned out that the climate change movement was full of classists. That might be a reason for working-class people to leave the movement – if only to avoid the unpleasantness of working with classists. But it doesn't seem to be any reason at all to reject climate change mitigation and adaptation as goals, or stop caring about climate change entirely and start caring about something else.

Hayden and King pointed to leftist men's endorsement of sex hierarchy. That is a problem with leftist men.[63] Jones wrote about women needing to stop fighting for the 'movement' and instead start fighting for their own liberation and independence. That is a problem with the 'movement' (the left), and of its projects and priorities not including women's liberation. Only radical women's reasons to leave *the left* are relevant to our question of whether feminism is an exclusively left-wing project. (If it's not left wing, then it's obviously not *exclusively* left wing.) Even if leftist men still, nearly sixty years later, naturalize women's 'difference' from men, implement a sexist division of movement labour, ignore and dismiss women's contributions to movement theory and strategy, sexualize and degrade women, fill all the important movement positions, and are only posturing as radicals, it could still be true that feminist women should be committed to the ideology of the left and only pursue women's equality (etc.) within those constraints, or that feminist women should work exclusively with the left *in* pursuing women's equality (etc.). (This is a distinction between whether feminists must themselves *be* leftists or only *work exclusively with* leftists.)

The other reasons are more at the core of the left. Set leftist men (and women, for that matter) aside: if feminism must be practised as identity politics, if the restructuring of the

The 1960s: Feminists Leaving the Left 33

relationship between the sexes requires some form of separatism, if to refuse to be made to wait until 'after the revolution' and if to refuse to have women's issues deprioritized *all make feminism distinct from and incompatible with the left*, then feminists even today have a reason to leave the left. It's not just the sexism of leftist men or the insistence of leftist women on prioritizing leftist issues over women's issues that's the problem; it's also what the left is considered to be against what feminism is. At the very least, we can say that one is about a lot more than women, even if it is also about women; and one is only about women. That may be enough for it to be clear that these are not the same project and so not obviously compatible. (A stronger claim would be that while the left speaks the language of universalism, it is really for men, so even when it champions minorities, it is really only championing minority men. That claim generates predictions, and so would be possible to assess empirically, but I won't take it up here.)

Jumping forward several decades, it is possible to extract an argument for feminism being a uniquely left-wing project from a somewhat surprising source: an evolutionary argument as to the origins of patriarchy.

Barbara Smuts has argued that an important component of the explanation of patriarchy – where 'Humans . . . exhibit more extensive male dominance and male control of female sexuality than is shown by most other primates'[64] – is social hierarchy *between men*. She suggests that, 'As a result of increasingly unequal relationships among men, women became increasingly vulnerable to the will and whims of the few most powerful men, and women's control over their own sexuality was greatly reduced'.[65] In evolutionary terms, where we hold fixed the interest of individuals in reproductive success, males will be unable to 'dominate and control' females without also dominating and controlling other males, because if they don't do the latter then those males will simply intervene with the

34   The 1960s: Feminists Leaving the Left

females. ('Thus, the coercive strategy will be unstable, and the most reproductively successful males will be those who compete by providing females with benefits that lead the females to voluntarily choose them as mates.')[66] Domination between males secures non-interference (or at least reduced interference).[67] In human societies, the greater the social inequality among men, the more that the men at the top can 'monopolize control over' women, partly because the men at the bottom have restricted access to resources so cannot intervene to offer them, and partly because the women are less free to choose their own partners, even if the less powerful men did have resources to offer.[68] 'Thus', Smuts concludes, 'the degree to which men dominate women and control their sexuality is inextricably intertwined with the degree to which some men dominate others.'[69]

This component of patriarchy, which Smuts summarizes as 'increased hierarchy formation among men', is just one of six factors that she thinks 'influenced the evolution of human gender inequality'.[70] In the conclusion to the paper, she says that all six factors 'point directly to the essential counter-strategies that women must develop in order to reduce gender inequality'.[71] For the other five factors, the counter-strategies are all things that can be pursued within a political movement *for* and *about* women. They include 'female political solidarity aimed at the creation of strong institutionalized protection of women from male violence and other forms of domination (such as changes in legislation related to rape and sexual harassment'); 'economic opportunities for women and ... legal protection of women's property rights'; the need to 'identify and change behaviours by women that contribute to patriarchy'; and 'the need for women to gain access to the media, the pulpit, the classroom, and government, in order to gain an equal voice for feminist ideology'.[72]

But there is one counter-strategy that takes feminists away from working *for* women, at least directly. Smuts writes, 'The

The 1960s: Feminists Leaving the Left 35

fourth factor – hierarchical relationships among men – emphasizes the need for women to support economic and political changes that will reduce inequality among men.'[73] Some feminists have been deeply hostile to the idea of working on men's issues and contemptuous towards the feminist women, especially, who have moved in that direction. If Smuts is right, then the reduction of inequality among men should be a commitment of feminism *because* this is part of what it takes to reduce men's control of women's sexuality and male dominance of women more generally. Men must be able to intervene against each other to make ever more attractive offers to women, and women must be free to choose among these offers. That requires conditions of equality, not hierarchy. And this gives us an argument for thinking about feminism as a left-wing project after all *to the extent that* the left is typically the side committed to social equality. (One way of distinguishing the left from the right is a concern with equality of outcome on the left, and equality of opportunity on the right – although in chapter 4 I'll take a more sceptical approach to this distinction.)[74] Still, it doesn't settle the 'working with' question; it could at best establish that feminism *is* left-wing, narrowing our question as to whether left-wing feminists should never/sometimes/always work with the right wing.

Is this a plausible way to think about men and women, and therefore about feminism and politics, in industrialized liberal democracies? Smuts notes that 'in all other primates, females rely on their own efforts to obtain food and do not depend on males for resources',[75] while, in humans, females have tended to secure access to resources *by* securing a male partner. But a woman can now work and be independent, and in welfare states under certain conditions she can even *not* work and still be independent. If she has children, things are more difficult – it remains challenging in most countries to be a single parent, work enough hours to support a family, and either have enough flexibility to simultaneously care for children or earn enough to cover institutionalized childcare. If the evolutionary factors that *explain* (the origins and persistence of) patriarchy do not remain in place, then this idea that feminism *now* must work against intra-male social hierarchy may be false, and so fail, after all, to provide an argument for feminism as an exclusively left-wing project.

Still, the general idea applies more broadly. If women's equality (etc.) will not be achieved solely by focusing on women's problems, or could be solved more quickly and efficiently by not focusing solely on women's problems, that may give feminists a reason to take a much wider set of actions as part of their 'work' (and so for us to take the much wider set of actions as the work one can do to count as a feminist). If this is work that is typically done by the left but not the right, that would provide a reason for feminists to work with the left and not the right.

It is clear that there are at least some cases where work *for* women means work *on* men. One example is the psychologist Kay Jackson, who worked in prisons with men incarcerated for rape.[76] This is (extremely difficult, personally challenging) work *for* women in the sense that it aims to reform rapists and make them less likely to reoffend against women upon release from prison. Suppose compelling empirical evidence suggested that economically desperate men – unemployed, underemployed, or in precarious work due to immigration status – were more likely to perpetrate domestic abuse against their wives and girlfriends. If that were the case, feminists would have a reason to support stronger social welfare protections and fairer immigration policies (something like, if the government is going to let people in, then it must let them work), *not* for their own sake but *because* of their downstream effects on women.

That some social policy will be 'good for women' in a vague, handwavy way does not give feminists a reason to support it or make supporting it 'feminist' work. Recall our definition from the end of chapter 1:

Feminist: a person who works for women's equality (whether of outcome or of opportunity), women's individual self-determination, women's liberation, or women's interests (as the person understands them, whether or not that is also as they are); or who works against male dominance.

These words, 'equality', 'self-determination', 'liberation', 'interests', all point to a *problem*: that there is *inequality* between the sexes, that women *lack* self-determination, that women are *not yet* liberated, that there are important interests women have that are *not yet* realized. Feminist work makes a contribution to solving these problems. If sex equality (etc.) had already been accomplished, then working hard for a stronger social safety net would not make a person a *feminist* just because women would be among the people helped by the implementation of a stronger social safety net. There needs to be both the background inequality that makes this work *for women* rather than merely work *for humans* (among which there are women), and there needs to be evidence for the connection between this policy and particular problems women face in conditions of sex inequality – like there was for domestic violence, in the hypothethical example given above.

In sum: 1960s radical women came out of the left, but left the left. Their reasons were not exhausted by leaving (sexist) leftist men. This shows there is no necessary connection between feminism and the left. Feminism can be, and some feminists believed it must be, independent of the left. *If* we can show that particular policies that are good for men or good for everyone address women's problems more efficiently, and the left is committed to those policies while the right isn't, that is some reason for feminists to work with the left. But it is a contingent and transient reason: if the left stopped being committed to those policies and the right started to be (which, as we will see in chapter 4, is perfectly possible), then feminists should *not* work with the left and *should* work with the right.

38 The 1960s: Feminists Leaving the Left

And, either way, the left at a time happening to be the side that is better for women doesn't remotely vindicate the stronger blanket claim that feminists should not work with the right. It might be that they *should* work with the right to get electoral politics to a point where all parties work for women.

Once we recognize that feminism is not an essentially leftist project, the issue of whether feminists should work with the left is just as much in question as whether feminists should work with the right – contrary to what is generally assumed today. (Because it's working with the right that is in question, I spend more time on it in the book, but I could just as well have added another chapter titled 'What's Wrong with the Left?', mirroring the approach taken in chapter 3.)

In the next chapter, we'll move from thinking about feminists and the left to thinking about feminists and the right.

3

What's Wrong with the Right?

A post to the subreddit r/AskFeminists in 2023 asks 'Why can't feminists be conservative?'[1] The poster explains that she has been a member of the subreddit community for a while but just came across the claim in its FAQs that feminists can't be conservative.[2] She says:

> that doesn't make much sense to me at all. I'm trained in economics and work in finance. I think capitalism is one of the best things that's happened to humanity because it's significantly increased everyone's standard of living (although not equally). Capitalism has done a lot for women, too. . . . Because I believe that capitalism improves people's lives more than government, I think government should stay as small as possible. Hence, I vote for small government, aka conservative. . . . How is being capitalist versus being socialist linked to being a feminist? I'm a feminist. I think women should have equal opportunities to men. Believing in equality doesn't mean I can't be a capitalist.

Her assumption seems to be that the progressive/conservative distinction is the socialist/capitalist distinction

– or at least, is the big government/small government distinction, which divides socialism from capitalism (whether it also describes other types of arrangements). Because she's pro-capitalist, she's for small government, and because she's for small government, she's conservative. Her question is why does that mean she can't be a feminist?

What's interesting about the replies is how many different characterizations of the conflict between feminism and conservatism they offer. Here are a few from within the ten most upvoted. Capitalism means meritocracy and meritocracy means hierarchy; patriarchal history puts men at the top of that hierarchy, and capitalism keeps them there. It's hard to square women's equality with inequality that favours men, and that is equivalent to it being hard to square feminism with conservatism. Feminism is progressive, and conservatism is the antithesis of progressivism. (I think the logic here – spelled out more fully in another reply – is that conservatism is about conserving, which means maintaining the status quo, while progressivism is about progress, which means reforming or changing the status quo. But conservatism about the status quo for the relation between the sexes would mean conserving male dominance, which is the antithesis of the progress against male dominance that feminism wants.) Feminism supports bodily autonomy while conservatism doesn't. (Again, the logic is not spelled out, but probably this poster is thinking of the feminism/conservatism distinction in terms of issues, and in particular the issue of abortion. Feminists are pro-choice and conservatives are pro-life goes the thought, so feminism and conservatism are not compatible.) One reply is careful to distinguish only *some* conservatism as being in tension with feminism, saying that social (but not economic) conservatives are anti-gay, anti-abortion, and pro-traditional family (while feminists, by implication, are pro-gay, pro-abortion, and either anti-traditional family or pro-alternative family arrangements and pro other choices than family for women).

Kathleen Stock, in an interview with Meghan Murphy about feminists allying with the right (Murphy 2019b), makes a similar distinction to that in the last reply: 'I am not saying, and I wouldn't want to say, that you should never ally with the right, given that the right is such a broad spectrum anyway. So I guess the people that I'm most concerned about allying with are potentially social conservatives, Christian fundamentalists, and also the far-right, the alt-right, people who have strong views about immigration.'[3] While she does not spell out the objection, it is presumably the sense that social conservatives and Christian fundamentalists oppose gay rights, and that the far right, the alt-right and anyone else with 'strong views about immigration' oppose multiculturalism (or are otherwise racist and/or xenophobic). It's not clear from Stock's comments whether she sees these as natural alliances for feminists to have – that feminism, gay rights and support for immigration 'go together', and, if so, why – or she sees these as feminist issues because they involve women – the lesbians protected by gay rights, the female migrants benefited by a more generous immigration quota and harmed by a more restrictive one. (An alternative, and perhaps more plausible, explanation of this comment is that Stock was talking about what *her* alliances should be, given *all* of her commitments, not limited to feminism. And that is a different question to what a feminist's alliances, qua feminist, should be.)

Could it be that opposition to feminists working with the right is based on a *conflation* of 'the right' with 'the religious right' or 'social conservatives', so that a lot of potentially advantageous alliances are being prohibited by a blanket moral imperative that has no real justification? Was Helen Joyce right that there's little more here than the idea that 'the right' is Sauron and the Orcs, and the Hobbits will steer clear if they know what's good for them?[4]

In this chapter, I'll focus on two ways of making plausible the objection to feminists working with the right. The first is issue based and focuses on the disagreement over abortion specifically. The idea is that some issues are so important that it's worth pursuing a 'single-issue' politics on their basis, and that this produces different results when it comes to who to work with and who not to work with than the standard approach would do. The second is about political co-opting, and says that precisely due to the predicament that *calls for* feminism, women will be used as pawns in men's political power games, and that reduces women's choice to which side to be used *by*. The left offers women a better deal, so women should opt for being used by the left rather than the right. Ultimately, I'll argue that neither of these arguments offers a successful vindication of the idea that feminists should not work with the right.

Here's a comment made by the British radical feminist Julie Bindel in the context of an UnHerd panel, 'Where Does Feminism Go Next?', along with Mary Harrington, Hadley Freeman and Sally Chatterton:

> I worry about some of the women in the US that are right-wing, that seem to not like trans people because they also don't like lesbians or gays. That are deeply conservative in a really not acceptable way. That are Trump supporters. That have this as a single issue, where they just shout about the trans and they'll go to the Heritage Foundation, and take an invitation from the worst kind of think tank, that also is looking to find ways to re-criminalize abortion. That worries me greatly, they're not my allies. So I won't join with them because they don't like the trans, because I could not give a damn about transgender people who should just be left alone to live their lives. As I said at the beginning, it's about our rights being erased. . . . when we've won this battle, I want the women who've only fought on the trans stuff to come and help us with the rape and domestic murder and stuff. . . . we'll be carrying on doing this because we

understand it's about women's liberation and not just a single issue.[5]

There's a clear *us and them* here, Bindel and her politics contrasted with 'right wing', 'deeply conservative', 'Trump supporters', 'they'll go to the Heritage Foundation', 'not my allies'. Abortion is mentioned – the Heritage Foundation is 'looking to find ways to re-criminalize abortion'. (Here Bindel is referring to the first of the dust-ups I mentioned in the Preface.) It's not entirely clear whether this reference to its stance on abortion is meant as a justification for *why* the Heritage Foundation is 'the worst kind of think tank' or as an independent reason for thinking that right-wing women cannot be Bindel's allies in feminism. But let's assume it's the latter, given our interest for now in explaining feminist left/right antagonism in terms of a single issue, namely abortion.

Abortion is an issue that has typically divided left from right. In the United States, the Republican Party platform in 2016 (before the overturning of *Roe v. Wade* in 2022) stated 'Through Obamacare, the [then-]current Administration has promoted the notion of abortion as healthcare. We, however, affirm the dignity of women by protecting the sanctity of human life.'[6] The 2020 Democratic Party platform, on the other hand, contains the statement, 'We believe unequivocally, like the majority of Americans, that every woman should be able to access high-quality reproductive health care services, including safe and legal abortion.'[7] House Republicans in March 2024 endorsed a national ban on abortion with zero exceptions (which is slightly strange, given that abortion in the United States is no longer a federal issue).[8]

Now that abortion has become a central political issue in the United States again, and given its importance as a *feminist* issue in particular, it makes sense that feminist women might take it as a reason to pick sides politically. We're looking for an argument against feminists working with the right; *that* the right (in the United States at least) opposes abortion then becomes a reason not to work with them. But it's worth noting that not *all* Democrats support legal abortion and not *all* Republicans oppose it. A survey done by Pew Research in 2022 looked into the Republicans who support it and the Democrats who oppose it, and found that 'Republicans who favour legal abortion are far less religious than abortion opponents in the GOP [Republican Party], while Democrats who say abortion should be illegal in all or most cases are much *more* religious than Democrats who say it should be legal.'[9] That suggests knowing someone's religion might be more useful than knowing their political party if the thing one cares about is their stance on abortion.

There's some messiness in my articulation of the issue above, both in referring to 'feminists' and in the slide from 'Republicans' to 'the right'. On the former, I've already argued, in chapter 1, that there can be right-wing and centrist feminists, yet the way I've phrased things above suggests that 'feminists' are *not* 'the right', that these are two distinct groups, one of which is considering whether to work with the other. On the latter, there are minor/third parties in the United States on the right of politics, including the Libertarian Party and the Constitution Party (so 'the right' is not exhausted by, and therefore not synonymous with, Republicans).[10] And there's at least a theoretical distinction between party and ideology, which came up in assessing feminists' reasons for leaving the left in chapter 2 (and on which more in chapter 4), meaning that one can have right-wing policy commitments without supporting a right-wing party, and one can support a right-wing party without having right-wing policy commitments. (In the first instance, one might think no party does an adequate job of representing those commitments; in the second instance, one might simply be in thrall to a charismatic leader.)

There's also a question about what *not working with* means. When people argue that feminists shouldn't work with the right, do they have in mind *voting for a party* (or supporting a party in other ways, such as leafletting and canvassing in the lead-up to an election), or something more diffuse, like working on specific projects *together with* people who vote for the Republican Party or support the party in other ways? Or do they have something *even more* diffuse in mind, like not working together with anyone who has right-wing policy commitments, even if what you're working together on has nothing to do with those commitments?

Maybe an articulation of the reason to not work with 'the right' in the name of abortion would help to resolve some of this messiness. That is, if we start from the claim that feminists shouldn't work with the right in the name of abortion, and then we try to come up with a charitable explanation of why that's true, we might land on a good enough reason to actually believe it. Let's start by thinking about left-wing, centrist, politically homeless and apolitical feminists refusing to work with right-wing feminists in terms of what that refusal communicates (and causes, if anything). Who is the refusal for? What does it communicate? Is the communication reliable? What do those who refuse to work with right-wing feminists get out of it, and what does their refusal do to right-wing feminists, or cause more generally?

Suppose that two feminist women are working at a women's homelessness shelter, one who has been employed there for a while, and one for whom it's her first day. Call the first woman – who let's suppose is a member of the United States' Green Party[11] – Greta, and the second woman – who let's suppose is a member of the Libertarian Party – Libby.

> *Greta and Libby.* Greta is chatting with Libby, and casually mentions a recent news article in a way that makes clear that she disapproves of pro-lifers. Libby discloses that she is herself a pro-lifer, at which point Greta abruptly walks away from the conversation. Libby is a little taken aback, but tries not to dwell

on it – perhaps Greta remembered something important that she needed to do, or perhaps Greta is just a bit odd socially. Later, Greta goes to the manager of the shelter and requests not to be rostered on to work with Libby again. She begins mentioning Libby's pro-life views to other volunteers, confidently expecting her disapproval to be shared.[12]

Who are the parties to Greta's refusal to work with Libby? They include Greta herself, obviously, and Greta's manager, as well as any fellow volunteers and women using the shelter who overhear Greta's conversations about Libby. (They'll include Libby herself, too, if the manager, one of the other volunteers or one of the women using the shelter informs Libby of what Greta has been saying.) What is being communicated by Greta's refusal to work with Libby is Greta's disapproval of pro-life views and any person with such views. The fact that she is not willing to continue talking with Libby, and requests not to be rostered on to work with Libby, suggests that she is not making a distinction between the person and her beliefs: Libby has pro-life beliefs, therefore Libby is a pro-lifer. *Libby*, not the beliefs, is the problem.[13] (Or Libby, so long as she has the beliefs, is the problem.) What does Greta get out of this? She gets to express her moral disapproval of pro-life views and the people who hold them. She also gets to show that she is willing to be vocal in her disapproval of others, that she refuses to adhere to norms of civility and mutual toleration – including in the workplace, where such behaviour could become a disciplinary matter – and that she is not conflict averse (at least, that she does not value social harmony over moral enforcement).

Finally, the most important question: is the communication reliable? One way to answer this question is to ask whether the communication is costly, with costliness being a proxy for reliability. This is a difficult matter because it partly depends on Greta's temperament. If Greta is not very sensitive to social norms and not very conflict averse by nature, then it is not costly to her to express disapproval, walk away from people mid-conversation, make unreasonable requests of managers, trash talk a colleague and violate social norms. If she *is* sensitive to social norms and is conflict averse, then these things might be quite costly (psychologically and emotionally). It also matters whether Greta's views are widely shared in the context in which she's refusing to work with Libby. If she knows the shelter is a left-dominated workplace, and so reasonably assumes that others will share her view about abortion, then it's not costly for her to uphold *their* moral and political orthodoxies. Indeed, this could be beneficial rather than costly, showing that she is one of the (moral/political) team. So only if it's a right-dominated (or, even better, religious-dominated) workplace *and* Greta is social norm sensitive and conflict averse can we clearly conclude that this behaviour is costly for her. And only if it's costly can we infer that it's reliable: that she really feels *so* strongly about abortion that these are the lengths she's willing to go to in its name. If it's not costly, there are too many other things it might be doing. (And even when it is costly, it might *still* be doing something other than revealing her real feelings – it might be a cost worth paying for some other objective she has, such as impressing a particular colleague whom she wants to date.)

(There's a complication here, to do with the reliability of *conformism*. The higher the penalties for dissent, the fewer dissenters there will be. So mere conformity is entirely unreliable as a guide to what people believe. In a high-conformity context, someone known to be insensitive to social norms may be the *more* reliable proxy, precisely because she will say what she thinks while others won't. So it's important to separate objective reliability from comparative reliability. An action may fail to be costly and therefore fail to secure reliability by that route, and yet we may judge it the most reliable of the available communications for other reasons.)

48 What's Wrong with the Right?

Considering Greta and Libby in detail shows that refusal to work with someone might be more of a punishment to the person excluded than it is a cost to the person doing the excluding. And that may cause confusion in third parties because it will look like a costly and therefore reliable communication: Greta must *really care* about abortion if she's unwilling to even be rostered on with Libby! But, in fact, being treated this way costs *Libby* a lot without necessarily being an accurate reflection of Greta's true feelings. It may be better conceived as a disproportionate punishment *of Libby* for something that Libby was fully entitled to do, namely to express disagreement with the view of a colleague being put forward in the workplace. (If it would be better for controversial topics to be kept out of the workplace, then this applies to both Greta and Libby, not just Libby.)

The stakes are extremely high on both sides of the abortion debate. Pro-lifers see the deaths of millions of babies[14]; pro-choicers see all the unwanted pregnancies, births and adoptions by women, and all the botched backdoor abortions women will seek when safe, legal abortions aren't available (and they have history to draw on to substantiate this claim). If there *is* a debate on which some views are considered 'beyond the pale' and therefore appropriate candidates for social alienation as reaction/retaliation/punishment, this is surely one of them. Yet my intuition, at least, is that Greta's behaviour is unacceptable. Greta is living in a liberal democracy in which people disagree about moral and political issues, and she should be able to interact civilly with people who disagree with her – even when they disagree about things that are very important to her.[15]

Perhaps my intuition is clouded by the fact that legal abortion is available and fairly secure in the country where I live. When you already *have* certain rights, and have them securely, you can afford to be sanguine about some people thinking you shouldn't have them. This suggests a difference between the homophobe in a country *with* equal marriage and adoption laws and in a country without them; between the pro-lifer in a state *without* abortion rights and in a state with them. In a country with equal marriage and adoption laws, the gay man can afford to be tolerant of those who would deny him equal rights; in a country without equal marriage and adoption laws, perhaps he cannot. (I'll set aside which of tolerance and intolerance is the more *effective* strategy for changing people's minds, and focus on how he is morally justified in responding.) In a state with abortion rights, a woman can afford to be tolerant of those who would deny her abortion rights; in a state without abortion rights perhaps she cannot. So whether Greta's behaviour is unacceptable depends on whether the state she lives in has secure abortion rights and not on her treatment of Libby per se.

An alternative way of assessing the case would be to use one of the most central liberal principles, specifically, the harm principle: we are only justified in interfering with another's conduct when it is harmful to others. Unfortunately, this doesn't mediate disagreement over abortion, which centres on *whether* there is harm to others (because there's a debate over when the 'person' begins and so whether the abortion of an embryo or foetus *is* the killing of a person).[16]

The Greta and Libby case takes *not working with* as interpersonal withdrawal in a workplace context, on the basis of a fellow employee's political views on a single issue. This kind of interpersonal disassociation is unfortunately commonplace today (not limited to the workplace). But there are other ways to understand *not working with the right* that may pack more punch than when 'the right' is taken to be an individual person with right-wing views. We might have considered, instead, whether the women's homelessness shelter should accept money from a prominent right-wing politician known to be opposed to abortion; whether, when the director of the shelter is offered an opportunity to speak about women and homelessness at a conservative conference platforming pro-pro-life speakers, she should accept the invitation; whether the shelter should accept volunteers from a local church whose religious doctrine opposes abortion; etc. For any such example, we can ask roughly the same set of questions we asked about Greta: who is the intended audience of a refusal, and what does it communicate; what does the shelter, or its director, get out of a refusal (or what does it cost it); and what does the refusal do to the politician, the conference (or its pro-life speakers specifically), or the church? It's easy to think of strategic considerations that point in favour of refusing, for example if donors were listed publicly and a consequence of accepting money from that particular politician would be other donors, who contribute more funding between them, withdrawing support. It's harder to think of principled reasons for why the shelter should refuse any of these things *even if* its director or some of its staff themselves have pro-choice views. There's just not enough of a connection between its core business, namely providing shelter to homeless women, and the abortion issue.

Earlier, I suggested that support for abortion divides the left from the right, albeit imperfectly (tracking religion *within* the left and right, at least in America). Suppose that *all* feminist women cared about was abortion, would that be a reason for them to support the left and refuse to work with the right? Andrea Dworkin, for one, appears to think the answer to this question is 'no'. The reason she gives relates to the *robustness* of leftist men's support for abortion rights for women, which she sees as being conditional on their usefulness to men in securing sexual access to women:

> It was the brake that pregnancy put on fucking that made abortion a high-priority political issue for men in the 1960s – not only for young men, but also for the older leftist men who were skimming sex off the top of the counterculture and even for more traditional men who dipped into the pool of hippie

girls now and then. The decriminalization of abortion – for that was the political goal – was seen as the final fillip: it would make women absolutely accessible, absolutely 'free'. The sexual revolution, in order to work, required that abortion be available to women on demand. If it were not, fucking would not be available to men on demand. Getting laid was at stake. Not just getting laid, but getting laid the way great numbers of boys and men had always wanted – lots of girls who wanted it all the time outside marriage, free, giving it away. The male-dominated Left agitated for and fought for and argued for and even organized for and even provided political and economic resources for abortion rights for women. The Left was militant on the issue.[17]

But she goes on to note that as feminism rose, with it so did women's clearer recognition of the ways in which they had been sexually used, including by the so-called 'revolutionaries'. As Dworkin, drawing on work by Robin Morgan, put it,

> the brother-lovers were sexual exploiters as cynical as any other exploiters – they ruled and demeaned and discarded women, they used women to get and consolidate power, they used women for sex and for menial labour, they used women up; . . . rape was a matter of utter indifference to these brother-lovers – they took it any way they could get it.[18]

Dworkin summed this up as 'this brave new radical wanted to be not only master in his own home but pasha in his own harem.'[19] And so the women left the men; they formed the feminist movement, independent from the leftist men. They 'found a first premise for their political movement: that freedom for a woman was predicated on, and could not exist without, her own absolute control of her own body in sex and in reproduction. This included not only the right to terminate a pregnancy but also the right to not have sex, to say no, to not be fucked.'[20]

52   What's Wrong with the Right?

Dworkin says of leftist men that 'most of them never recognized feminism except in terms of their own sexual deprivation; feminists were taking away the easy fuck'. And she sees this as tied to a withdrawal of support for abortion: 'Material resources dried up. Feminists fought the battle for decriminalized abortion – no laws governing abortion – on the streets and in the courts with severely diminished male support.'[21] She even goes so far as to say that, 'The leftist men turned from political activism: without the easy lay, they were not prepared to engage in radical politics.'[22]

> The male left abandoned abortion rights for genuinely awful reasons: the boys were not getting laid; there was bitterness and anger against feminists for ending a movement (by withdrawing from it) that was both power and sex for the men; there was also the familiar callous indifference of the sexual exploiter – if he couldn't screw her she wasn't real.[23]

And even though Dworkin wrote this in 1983, it seems just as relevant to the United States today:

> The hope of the male Left is that the loss of abortion rights will drive women back into the ranks – even fear of losing might do that; and the male Left has done what it can to assure the loss. The Left has created a vacuum that the Right has expanded to fill – this the Left did by abandoning a just cause, by its decade of quietism, by its decade of sulking. But the Left has not just been an absence; it has been a presence, outraged at women's controlling their own bodies, outraged at women's organizing against sexual exploitation, which by definition means women also organizing against the sexual values of the Left. When feminist women have lost legal abortion altogether, leftist men expect them back – begging for help, properly chastened, ready to make a deal, ready to spread their legs again. On the Left, women will have abortion on male terms, as part of sexual

What's Wrong with the Right? 53

liberation, or women will not have abortion except at risk of death.[24]

If we really wanted to lean into Dworkin's claim as an objection to thinking of abortion as robustly protected by the left, we'd need empirical evidence substantiating her claim about radical men abandoning support for abortion and even radical politics entirely when sexual access to women ceased to be guaranteed. That is evidence I don't have and am not sure how to get. So we can just take it as something to consider: *if* Dworkin is right, then the connection between abortion rights for women and the left is considerably less robust than has been supposed, and that means even a single-issue preoccupation with abortion cannot justify a blanket prohibition on working with the right. (If the right were to become more supportive of abortion, which could happen simply as a matter of the religious right becoming a dwindling proportion *of* the right, then feminists with a single-issue focus on abortion should work with the right.)

It is worth acknowledging, of course, that many feminists would reject taking a 'single-issue' approach to politics for the reason that this may mean sacrificing too much when it comes to other issues at the time (which together may add up to more than the value of the single issue) and also risking too much when it comes to other issues over the longer term. My concern at the moment is *in principle* reasons not to work with the right, using a single-issue focus on abortion as one example. That does not preclude strategic considerations about which of left and right are likely to be better on all issues of concern to women, both at a time and over time. We'll return to those more strategic considerations in chapter 6.

Not long after I first 'came out' as a gender-critical feminist, I was at a conference in Boston where two feminist philosophers took me aside to – as I'm sure they saw it – attempt to talk some sense into me about my stance on trans women. One, the more senior of the two, implored me not to allow myself to be a useful idiot for the right. (I'm pretty sure she didn't use that term, but I can't remember exactly how she put it.) The right opposes men claiming to be women, so if *I* oppose men claiming to be women, then I'm doing the work of the right and making it possible for them to use me as a kind of shield: 'Hey, look, even feminists agree with us about trans women!' I remember being polite and hearing her out but privately wondering why she thought *I* was the one being used. After all, couldn't the same be said about her and *her* stance on trans women? Didn't her acceptance of men's claims to be women make *her* a useful idiot *for the left* in their infinite quest for freedom, even from the body and biological sex itself? Wasn't there something embarrassing about a self-declared feminist who couldn't say 'no' to leftist men insisting that some of their comrades *really are women*? Aren't they the ones using feminists like *her* as a shield?

There's a more sophisticated rendering of my inchoate sense of indignation at the moralizing of this senior feminist philosopher to be found in a paper about the militant suffragette Christabel Pankhurst, written by the historian Nicoletta Gullace. Gullace explains that both Christabel and Emmeline Pankhurst 'adopted an extreme patriotic agenda because it was the most expedient way to promote their feminist ideals'.[25] They relied on a comparison with (some) men that would show women to be more deserving of the vote: 'The Pankhursts' patriotic endorsement of stern war measures, their gigantic parades in favour of replacing male with female labour, and their xenophobic denunciation of German spies, pacifists, and naturalized British subjects were all designed to demonstrate the superiority of female citizenship over that of men and "half-men" who refused to support the war effort.'[26] Here the contrast with men is made clear: 'The lynchpin to the suffragettes' self-fashioning during the Great War was to repeatedly draw attention to the loyalty, bravery, and hardheaded militancy of disenfranchised British women, in comparison to the cosmopolitanism, pacifism, and socialism of a host of men, such as Liberals, union men, or conscientious objectors, who were enfranchised only because of their sex.'[27]

While the Pankhursts' interest was in demonstrating women's deservingness of the franchise, especially compared with some of those who already had it, their tactics made them appealing to conservative men for other reasons:

> The Women's Party itself and the effectiveness of right-wing feminism in winning the vote during the war, I would argue, offer clues to the enduring appeal of conservative feminism in the English-speaking world. ... harnessing the feminine mystique to nationalism, xenophobia, and anti-bolshevism could enhance their personal status, undercut their enemies, and melt much of the opposition to female citizenship. As women, particularly as *attractive* women (even in their later years), Christabel and Emmeline Pankhurst could be instrumental in embarrassing men whose policies, whether liberal, internationalist, pacifist, or socialist, seemed less virile than their own. For this reason, right-wing women became an almost irresistible temptation for right-wing men who wished to show up their more liberal peers.[28]

It's no accident, then, that Christabel was embraced by conservatives, winning a coveted conservative political endorsement and being celebrated in the right-wing media.[29] But as it is told here, the temptation to right-wing men is to *show up liberal men*, not to support the women's cause.

Even if this worked to the Pankhursts' ends in the case described, there is an argument against working with the right that can be extracted here. It goes something like this. For historical reasons (patriarchy and the male dominance it established), politics is conducted mainly between men – that was certainly true at the time of the suffragettes but, given the extent to which men still dominate political life, it may still be true. Thus women, even when acting for their own political ends, will be co-opted to men's political projects. The Pankhursts made left-wing men look bad, so they were accepted by right-wing men. But if right-wing men don't actually *support* the feminist project and merely instrumentalize feminists insofar as that helps them with their own projects, including opposition to left-wing men, then in aligning with right-wing men feminists are merely allowing themselves to be used *for* right-wing men's ends. Knowing that this is the case, feminists should assess which side's ends are better and worse for women. The left is better for women than the right, *therefore* feminists should refuse to work with – or, really, be co-opted by – the right.

One objection to this line of reasoning is that it privileges men's agency over women's. The Pankhursts were acting strategically to secure women the vote. They did so brilliantly, and they ended up converting a number of conservative men to the women's cause. Just as I wondered privately about the reasoning of the senior feminist philosopher and why it couldn't be reversed against her, we may wonder on behalf of Christabel why anyone should think that *she* was being used by conservative men, rather than that *she was using* conservative men. She knew what she was doing; she was no one's useful idiot. Another objection might be that it doesn't matter *why* people support a cause, only *that* they support it. Should Christabel have been concerned to discover that some proportion of the conservative men who supported women's suffrage were just gleeful about being able to show some women to be more patriotic and tougher than the progressive men they opposed on other issues? I'm tempted to say she shouldn't, although it's worth conceding that the support of such men is more *robust* when they genuinely agree with the cause rather than merely see some temporary or contingent benefits from supporting it.

Yet another objection is that the left is *not* better for women. It is better on some issues and worse on others. We've already discussed one issue that it is arguably *currently* better on, namely abortion, and considered Dworkin's view that leftist men's commitment to abortion rights for women is far less robust than it may appear. But it is also worse on a number of issues, at least relative to a radical feminist perspective, including surrogacy, prostitution, pornography and sex/gender identity. It's at least non-obvious whether more women are harmed in the making of pornography and in the course of sex work now than were harmed by the lack of availability of abortion in the past, for example. If we were to really weigh up all the harms of all the things the left and right are good and bad at when it comes to women's issues, I for one find it difficult to predict which side would emerge the victor.

A fourth (and final) objection is that now that women have the vote, thanks to the efforts of women like the Pankhursts, it is not plausible to think that they will only ever be co-opted by political men, and must choose the lesser evil to be co-opted by. As half the population, women are a significant lobby group capable of advocating for their interests to be represented by *any* party *anywhere* on the political spectrum. Even if it were true that the left were the lesser evil when it comes to women's issues, there's no reason to take such a defeatist line as thinking that the left's and the right's *current stances* on women's issues are fixed matters between which women can only choose the least bad. So the likelihood of political co-optation does not, after all, provide a convincing argument for feminists refusing to work with the right.

The arguments in this chapter are not decisive in establishing that feminists have no good reason to refuse to work with the right because they are not exhaustive. I talked about abortion as one policy issue that tends to divide left and right, but there are many such candidate issues, and each would require its own discussion. Stock mentioned immigration. To fill this out a bit, suppose a feminist were to say that because she cares about women's interests in conditions of global sex inequality, the policy issue she's most passionate about is immigration, and, in particular, refugee and asylum-seeker policy. Women in poorer and more violent countries do very badly, so she's insistent about doing whatever is possible to increase the flow of women *out of* such countries and into countries like her own where they'll have more opportunities and be safer. The right-wing parties in her country have a worse track record on refugee and asylum-seeker policy, so she sticks with the left-wing parties. Some of what I said about abortion, including about the robustness of its association with the left, will generalize to immigration (and other issues), but some won't.

Specific women who oppose feminists working with the right may have specific concerns that I have failed to imagine here. Some of these may emerge in the next chapter, where we turn to the question of what 'the left' and 'the right' actually mean. If we can fill this out a bit more, it may become obvious *what* of the right feminists have reason to oppose. (And not merely oppose, but oppose where opposition to which justifies comprehensive political disassociation.)

4

The Myth of Left and Right

I said at the start of chapter 1 that there are a lot of moving parts in the claim *feminists should not work with the right*. We've talked about *feminists* and we've touched on *working with* (although there's more to be said in chapter 5), which leaves one final part to lock down, namely *the right*. You will have noticed that I've made frequent reference to 'the left' and 'the right', without ever saying precisely what I mean. That was intentional: I think different people mean different things by these terms, and I don't see it as a particularly helpful assessment of the target claim to simply say, *here's what I mean by 'the right', and on that meaning, if feminists want to work with the right they should knock themselves out.* In this chapter, though, we tackle the question head on.

Let's start by assessing a rather bold claim, put forward recently by a political scientist and historian duo: we *can't* fix the meaning of 'the left' and 'the right' because the whole idea of a left/right political spectrum is 'a lot of sound and fury signifying nothing'.[1] If 'the left' and 'the right' are empty concepts, then there can be no useful answer to the question of whether feminism is an exclusively left-wing project or whether feminists should work with the right. And, if they are

60 The Myth of Left and Right

empty concepts, that would change the direction of this book; instead of seeking an answer as to *why* feminists shouldn't work with the right, we'd need to turn to explanations of *what* the discourse about feminism and the right is actually doing. (If it's not *referring* to anything real, then it must have some other function, perhaps as political propaganda, perhaps as individual virtue-signalling, perhaps something else.)

In their book *The Myth of Left and Right*, brothers Hyrum and Verlan Lewis pit a social theory of left/right against what they call an essentialist theory of left/right, and they mobilize considerable evidence against the essentialist theory.[2] According to the social theory, people form tribes, and tribes adopt policy issues. The issues may not be connected in any other way than that they are held by a particular tribe, and the issues held by a particular tribe may change radically over time. Individuals join (or remain members of) tribes for social reasons, and generally go along with whatever their tribe is doing.

According to the essentialist theory, on the other hand, people adopt – or find themselves drawn to as a matter of conscience – particular principles. These principles entail sets of policy issues, issues which are connected to each other by the underlying principles. People form groups on the basis of shared principles and support political parties that do a good enough job of representing those principles by adopting the policy positions entailed by them. So long as an individual's commitment to the underlying principles doesn't change, her policy commitments shouldn't change, and neither should her allegiance to the party doing the best job of representing them. Should a party *cease* to do a good job of representing them, though, we should expect to see the individual follow the principle and not the party, for example moving to support a new party that does a better job in representing the principles she's committed to.[3] And, of course, if her principles do change, then we should similarly expect to see her move to support whichever party does the best job of representing them.

The Myth of Left and Right 61

According to the essentialist theory of left/right, the concepts of 'the left' and 'the right' are *timeless* (they have referred to the same principles at different times), *universal* (they refer to the same principles everywhere, rather than referring to different principles for different people who invoke them, including for people in different countries), and *unchanging* (the principles and the policy positions entailed by those principles are static, rather than malleable or evolving).[4] Lewis and Lewis argue against the essentialist theory by showing that none of these three requirements is met.

First of all, the concepts of 'the left' and 'the right' are not timeless. They were an invention of the French Revolution, later taken up in Russia by the Bolsheviks, and which made their way to the United States in the 1920s (Lewis and Lewis: ch. 3). They have been used to characterize American politics for only about 100 years. (The 'left'/'right' concepts are also used elsewhere, obviously, including in the United Kingdom, Australia and New Zealand – but *The Myth of Left and Right* presents evidence relating exclusively to the United States.) At their inception, they referred to a disagreement over the extent of authority of King Loius XVI, with the 'anti-royalist revolutionaries' seated on the left of the presiding officer in the National Assembly, and the 'aristocratic supporters of the monarchy' seated to the officer's right.[5]

Even within the period of a few years, the same concepts were used to refer to different things. For example, 'the right', represented by Republicans, 'as late as 1952' wanted small government, then during the 1950s 'began to break with their small government principles in the name of rooting out communist subversion', supporting 'government infringements on privacy, civil liberties, and free speech, believing that this sacrifice of freedom was necessary to preserve a free government from communist overthrow'.[6] Or 'the left', represented by Democrats, was fiercely *for* free speech during the same period (the McCarthy era) but is today against it, supporting

62   The Myth of Left and Right

restrictions on speech in the name of protecting minorities.[7] There are many other examples in the book.

In some countries, the authors say, 'the left' and 'the right' refer to just one issue, like the Israel/Palestine issue in Israel (or perhaps Scottish Independence in Scotland in past years), while in others, including the United States, the concepts refer to many issues.[8] And, finally, the issues belonging to 'the left' appear to change over time to such an extent that an issue can entirely flip from 'left' to 'right'. One dramatic example is isolationism versus interventionism when it comes to foreign policy. In World War I, World War II and the Korean War, 'the left' (Democrats) was *for* intervention and 'the right' (Republicans) was opposed.[9] Post-Vietnam War, 'the left' approached pacifism.[10] The 1972 Democratic presidential candidate 'ran on an explicitly anti-war platform'.[11] By 2004, a substantially greater proportion of 'conservatives' (Republicans) supported the Iraq War than 'liberals'.[12] While conservatives under Bush were interventionist, conservatives under Trump were isolationist.[13] As Lewis and Lewis put it:

> The right-wing reversal on foreign policy happened with remarkable suddenness. Almost as soon as Bush left office, conservatives came to believe (even more than liberals) that America intervenes too much in the affairs of other nations. As tribal leadership on the right passed from interventionist George W. Bush to isolationist Donald Trump, the views of rank-and-file conservatives changed accordingly. Conservatives supported the War in Iraq in much higher numbers than liberals, not because the War aligned with conservative *principles* but because it aligned with conservative *people*.[14]

You may have noticed that 'the left', 'liberals', 'progressives' and 'Democrats' are being used interchangeably, as are 'the right', 'conservatives' and 'Republicans'. That's deliberate. For if the essentialist theory is false and the social theory is true,

The Myth of Left and Right 63

then there is no underlying principle that could provide the basis of a meaningful distinction between principle and party.

Lewis and Lewis are arguing that the essentialist theory *is* false. As we can see from the examples just given, 'the left' and 'the right' are *not* timeless, universal or unchanging. There is no principle that rationalizes the set of policy issues associated with 'the right', which, had there been, might at least have provided reason to consider *change* as *progress* (towards an ideal). Lewis and Lewis go through a number of possible underlying principles that have been thought to explain the distinction between left and right, for example 'change vs. preservation', 'collectivism vs. individualism', 'equality vs. hierarchy', 'equality vs. liberty', 'idealism vs. realism' and 'simple vs. complex'. They argue that none of these succeed in distinguishing left from right, or rationalizing and connecting the various policy positions associated with each.[15] (Unfortunately, they do not consider equality of outcome versus equality of opportunity, which would at least have distinguished two of the definitions of feminism from chapter 1 in left/right terms. But given that Lewis and Lewis dismiss *all* the candidates they consider, we can presume that they would dismiss that one too.)

Without an underyling principle that rationalizes the associated policy issues, we cannot draw a meaningful distinction between principle and party (where Republicans could be criticized for failing to live up to conservative principles), and we cannot point to anything *about* 'the right' that is timeless, universal and unchanging – and the same goes for 'the left'. There are *only* two 'teams' or 'tribes', each with a motley collection of unrelated policy issues, and which drop some issues and pick up other issues over time. Lewis and Lewis recommend that we simply stop using these terms, and start talking in terms of 'tribe left' or 'team blue', or just using party labels.[16] This forces us to acknowledge our tribalism rather than hiding it with terms suggestive of deep principled commitments. As the authors put it:

essentialism allows people to conform to everything their party does while convincing themselves that they are being rational, principled, and philosophical instead of emotional, tribal, and conformist. Americans socialized into 'team left' or 'team right' take the issue positions they do because they are falling in line with their party, but essentialism lets them believe that they take these particular positions because they are following a philosophy.[17]

If this is all true, then the feminists who claim to be speaking from the left against feminists working with the right are doing nothing but hanging out with their group of pals and yelling at another group of pals that they don't like them. Everyone who does this should be embarrassed. So, *is* it all true?

Lewis and Lewis are not always as charitable about individuals as they could be. One can easily get the impression from their book that *everyone* is an ideologue, attached to party and uncaring about principle, mindlessly going along with whatever policy positions their party takes and yet using high-minded language in order to obscure the extent of their tribal behaviour from themselves and others. *Everyone* self-describing as a 'conservative' or 'of the right' is really just a Republican happy to do whatever the Republicans are doing, and *everyone* self-describing as a 'liberal' or 'progressive', or 'of the left', is really just a Democrat happy to do whatever the Democrats are doing.

The most the authors seem prepared to concede is that there are some 'sticky ideologues', people 'so attached to a particular iteration of their ideology that they resist going along with subsequent transformations'.[18] Here's Stock again, from the interview with Meghan Murphy, mentioned already, about feminists allying with the right:

> There's no one thing, really, that's easily defined to say what the left is. Or the right. So, the left, especially in America, quite often

The Myth of Left and Right   65

people describe themselves as on the left in America and I just do not recognize – it looks so individualistic and material and capitalist. I just think, in what sense are you, really, interested in traditional left-wing things? Except that you're into identity politics, which I don't see as a central part of left politics at all.[19]

She puts this in a way compatible with the social theory. Perhaps the left really does mean different things in the United States compared to the United Kingdom. Perhaps *traditional* leftism is collectivist and anti-capitalist, and *contemporary* leftism is individualistic and pro-capitalist. But with a few minor tweaks we can make Stock into a 'sticky ideologue' (in order to illustrate Lewis and Lewis's point): *real* leftism for Stock is the version she met in her twenties; when other leftists changed, she stood still. (And she's hardly the only one – an issue of the *Radical Notion* blasting non-partisan feminists for risking fascism invokes class struggle incessantly.)[20] That doesn't make her more principled than the leftists today obsessed with identity politics; it just makes her loyal to another, equally not essentialist, iteration of leftism. Lewis and Lewis offer us tribalists and sticky ideologues, but no one with real political principles.[21]

There are some reasons for caution about this view of individuals. The first is that some of the evidence Lewis and Lewis introduce to argue against essentialism actually seems to work *for* individuals being principled rather than tribal (even if what they are principled *about* is a single issue, or a principle that does not connect all, or even most, of the issues of their party – more on which soon). They give as evidence of 'the left' and 'the right' changing over time the fact that the demographics supporting each party – Democrat and Republican – have changed over time:

During the New Deal era, educated and wealthy Americans in urban areas overwhelmingly identified as Republican and were

66 The Myth of Left and Right

considered 'right-wing', while working-class Americans in rural areas overwhelmingly identified as Democratic and were considered 'left wing'. In the twenty-first century, the demographic bases of the two parties have completely switched. Working-class whites in the Rust Belt and Appalachia, who had been part of the 'left wing' Democratic Party coalition during the mid-twentieth century, now vote for, and identify with, the 'right-wing' Republican Party. This social divide between urban coastal elites and working-class whites in 'flyover country' is a dominant dividing line in American politics. *Despite this massive shift in the demographic bases of the two parties, the ideological labels remain the same: those demographic groups associated with the Democratic Party were previously considered 'liberals', but now that they are associated with the Republican Party they are considered 'conservatives'.* The people and their values haven't changed substantially, but the ideologies have. Demographic groups who were standing still in their priorities and commitments now find themselves in the opposite tribe.[22]

But if the tribal hypothesis were true, we'd expect such individuals to *retain* their party identifications and simply roll along with the associated policy changes, rather than stand still and lose their party identifications to the point that where they were once 'liberals', they are now 'conservatives'. If the people stand still and the parties change around them, then the people may be principled and the parties not; there's no reason to conclude that the people are not principled and merely going along mindlessly with their parties.

Furthermore, although Lewis and Lewis elsewhere in their book *object* to the idea of 'left-wing' people standing still and 'the left' leaving them on the grounds that *there is no 'the left'* and so no 'leftwards' direction to be left for, there clearly is a phenomenon of standing still while being left by others who were on your team, and of your party representing you

The Myth of Left and Right 67

adequately at one time and then failing to represent you adequately at another time.[23] We can put this in terms other than 'the left left me!', for example to say, 'Other people who think of themselves as "the left" started caring about something that I think is really stupid!', and, 'My party used to care about things I care about, but now it is completely obsessed with a topic I hate!', but there is nonetheless something to talk about here, and that 'something' will be of particular relevance in thinking about the connection between feminism and the commonly invoked left/right spectrum.

An alternative explanation to people just going along with their parties *no matter what* is that the reason people subscribe to parties is dependent on one or two issues that are important to them. If that were true, it would be compatible with the empirical evidence showing that people follow their parties through substantial changes in policy positions, *so long as* the party doesn't move on the issues most important to them. But to test *that* hypothesis, we'd need to know which issues were most important to each person, and also to track when and whether they changed their minds on those issues (because if someone has a genuine change of mind on a policy issue, it shouldn't be surprising that they'll stay with a party that now represents their new view on that issue). On this view, it's not that the concepts of 'the left' and 'the right' are *empty* and 'mythological', but rather that they are *capacious*, allowing each person to refer to the specific issue or set of issues they care about, and every other person to refer with the same words to a *different* specific issue or set of issues.

Lewis and Lewis object to thinking about 'the left' and 'the right' as capacious rather than empty on the grounds that there is no such thing as a private language. They write: 'Those who believe that Trump supporters are fake conservatives assume that the term "conservative" has a meaning independent of its public usage, but words are public by nature. We use them to communicate with others and to use a private definition

68   The Myth of Left and Right

of a word that is at variance with its public usage results in confusion.'[24]

This objection is certainly fair in some cases. For example, if I'm in the United States, where the shared meaning of 'egg' (at least in ordinary contexts)[25] is the thing laid by chickens that is high in protein and can be ordered for breakfast poached, scrambled, folded or fried, then it would be peculiar of me to go about insisting that what *I* mean by 'egg' is someone who is a bit of an idiot (which, by the way, is what New Zealanders often mean by it). But it's not fair in all cases. In particular, it's not fair in cases of *contested terms*.

Take 'Australian', for example. When someone self-describes as 'Australian', does that mean they were born in Australia? Are a citizen of Australia? Live in Australia and plan to stay, regardless of formal residency status? Feel a connection to or affinity with Australia, more so than any other country? Has one parent born in Australia, even if they've never visited? What about when someone says something like, 'She's *so* Australian'. What does that mean? Saying that the meaning of some terms is contested is not the same thing as saying that anyone departing from dominant usage is guilty of using a private language. Sometimes people use language differently in order to change or expand the meaning of terms. Suppose, for example, that at one time 'Australian' referred only to those with Australian citizenship, but then non-citizens living long-term in Australia began to express that they felt marginalized by this usage, and so some people began using the term in a more expansive way.

If we accepted the private-language argument for all contested terms, we'd end up being status quo biased, for whatever the dominant meaning is would settle the matter of what the term meant, and anyone wanting to expand or reform the meaning of the term would have no alternative but to introduce a *new* term. One term that is obviously contested is 'feminism' (or 'feminist'), with different groups of women

The Myth of Left and Right   69

using the term in different ways, but all fighting for *their* meaning to become *the* meaning. This is not a 'private language' but a public contest. Why not think the same applies to 'the left' and 'the right', people having different views about what is key to these concepts, and fighting to settle the meaning of the concepts publicly? Perhaps the answer is that feminists acknowledge the contestation and so tend to go to lengths to explain what they mean, while invocations of 'left' and 'right' imply a settled content that Lewis and Lewis are right to point out just can't be found.

If we accept Lewis and Lewis's argument that there is no left/right political spectrum, just parties and the policy issues they happen to have at a time, these are our options for thinking about feminists who claim that feminism is an exclusively left-wing project or that feminists shouldn't work with the right:

- They are Democrat (Labour/Green) loyalists, whose tribal attachments are producing the irrational behaviour of pursuing a politics *for women* while dividing women into an 'us' and a 'them' and refusing to work with women from the 'them' side.
- They are 'sticky ideologues' with an attachment to a previous version of a Democrat (Labour/Green) platform; they believe that what is good *for women* follows from, or is at least compatible with, this platform and will not work with anyone whose ideology is different or incompatible with that platform.[26]

These two groups include feminists whose preoccupation with theory (e.g., Marxism in the 1960s through to the 1980s) comes at the expense of their acknowledgement of the realities of political movements. Regardless of whether there is some perfect version of 'the left' that an individual can name, all that exists in reality is a messy and imperfect political movement made up of real people who may in reality be quite hostile to

70 The Myth of Left and Right

women and women's interests (as per the discussion in chapter 2). Feminists' decisions about who to vote for, donate to, campaign for, lobby and 'work with' more generally must be made on a political, not a merely theoretical, basis.

If we accept, instead, that the concepts 'left' and 'right' may be *capacious* rather than *empty*, we can add this further explanation of what's going on with feminists who claim that feminism is an exclusively left-wing project, or that feminists shouldn't work with the right:

- They feel most strongly about a principle or policy position that Democrats (Labour/Green) are currently adequately representing, are willing to go along with the rest of the party platform while this remains the case, and are unwilling to work with anyone opposed to that principle or policy position.

The last of these explanations is in line with one of the recommendations Lewis and Lewis make for moving forward in light of the fact that the left/right political spectrum is, in their view, a myth. The recommendation is to 'go granular'.[27] As they put it:

> Since political positions do not come naturally packaged together, we should stop pretending they do. Instead of thinking in terms of left and right, we should think in terms of specific policies and ideas, such as 'income tax increase', 'abortion rights', 'deficit reduction', 'affirmative action', or 'free trade'. We should replace meaningless ideological categories, such as 'liberal' or 'conservative', with substantive categories, such as 'deficit hawk', 'tax cut advocate', 'immigration restrictionist', or 'abortion rights activist'.[28]

If feminists 'go granular' about what it is in the Democrat/ Republican platform they really care about, this should make

The Myth of Left and Right

it easier to work out *whether* they can consistently work with others who disagree with them on that issue (if they're both working together to pursue a *different* issue, there may be no tension at all), and *why* there would be any reason not to work with others who disagree.

Suppose a Democrat-supporting feminist's hill-to-die-on is abortion rights, and she will not work with anyone who opposes abortion rights out of a fear that doing so will strengthen their hand. If she is clear that *this* is the issue (and, this is the *only* issue) that makes her prepared to refuse to work with some women, that will save her from cutting off a huge number of 'conservative' or 'right-wing' women who *don't* oppose abortion rights. If we can all get clear on what we really care about, and think about whether it's actually true that working together with specific others will 'strengthen their hand',[29] there might be many more productive strategic alliances.

5

Ethical versus Political Reasons to Not 'Work With'

In this chapter, we'll set aside that our specific interest in this book is in *feminists* working with *the right* in favour of considering the more abstract and general moral issue of 'working with' others. Once we have a sense of the moral issues, we can apply our thinking back to the specific question of feminists and the right. (Or, as per the last chapter, feminists and Republicans – feminists and 'team red'.)

Before we start, a clarification about how I'm understanding 'working with'. Sometimes people will accuse their ideological opponents of *working with* others when they merely share the same ends, even if they have very different reasons for them. If a religious fundamentalist opposes child medical transition because she wants to protect the child's ability to grow up and participate in the heterosexual nuclear family, and a gender-critical feminist opposes child medical transition because she wants to preserve heterogeneity in expressions of femaleness, they have the same ends, but different reasons. If they both work for their ends, but otherwise do not collaborate in any way, then they are not *working together*. Working independently for the same ends is not 'working together', even if the work of each group helps the other to get what they want.

This distinction is important because the idea that people are working together is often weaponized in order to get one group to change its ends (or its reasons, and so its ends). When other feminists accuse gender-critical feminists of 'working with religious fundamentalists' because they both want to stop childhood medical transition, their aim is to get the gender-critical feminists to stop opposing childhood medical transition. There is not actually a substantive objection to people working together – people are not working together in the first place. There is nothing of moral substance beyond the mere dislike of the end that is worked for. To apply this point to the dust-ups mentioned in the Preface, there *was* working together between feminists and the Heritage Foundation in 2019 (in the form of accepting a venue and host); there *wasn't* working together between feminists and white supremacists in Melbourne in 2023; there *was* working together between feminists and the National Workers Alliance in 2024 (in the sense of accepting equipment and sharing a platform); and there *wasn't* working together between feminists and fascists/racists/xenophobes at a rally against two-tier policing in the United Kingdom in 2024.[1]

So the first thing we need to do when faced with an accusation involving 'working with' is to ask *whether there is in fact working together going on*. Only if there is will the rest of this chapter be relevant.

Bear with me for a moment while I reintroduce an influential idea from the second wave of feminism, which will be helpful to us in addressing the issue of this chapter. 'The Personal Is Political' was the title of a memo written by Carol Hanisch in February 1969, circulated within the Women's Liberation Movement in the United States at the time, and published in *Notes from the Second Year* in 1970. Hanisch was responding to the criticism of consciousness-raising groups that they are 'therapy', and not political, as well as claims by leftist men and

74   Reasons to Not 'Work With'

some women that a lot of what was on the women's liberation agenda was 'personal', not political.

In consciousness-raising groups, women came together to talk about their lives and their experiences, to find common patterns. A woman who thought she had an individual problem of a violent husband might thereby discover that she was part of a group experiencing male violence against women and girls. Some said this was mere 'personal therapy' and 'navelgazing'.[2] Feminists put 'body issues' like 'sex, appearance and abortion', and domestic issues like the unequal distribution of household labour, onto the women's liberation agenda.[3] Some said that body issues were 'personal problems', and that domestic labour was for each woman to work out with her partner – she just needed to 'stand up for [herself]' and 'take more responsibility for [her] own [life]'.[4]

Hanisch pushed back on these criticisms, writing, 'One of the first things we discover in these groups is that personal problems are political problems. There are no personal solutions at this time. There is only collective action for a collective solution.'[5] That is, consciousness-raising meetings *gave her* a political understanding:

> I went, and I continue to go to these meetings because I have gotten a political understanding which all my reading, all my 'political discussions', all my 'political action', all my four-odd years in the movement never gave me. I've been forced to take off the rose-coloured glasses and face the awful truth about how grim my life really is as a woman. I am getting a gut understanding of everything as opposed to the esoteric, intellectual understanding and *noblesse oblige* feelings I had in 'other people's' struggles.[6]

If women think their situation is a 'personal problem', then they will blame themselves for their failures.[7] If they see their predicament as one that is imposed upon them *as women*, they will see that only collective political action can change their circumstances. The same point applies to solutions: if the problem is the social expectation that women wear make-up, and this expectation is bad for all women (spending money on products and time on application that men don't have to spend, and participating in their own objectification, which men do not suffer the indignity of), then the solution is not for *one woman to stop wearing make-up*, or to *treat badly another woman who wears make-up*. Political problems do not have individual solutions.

Hanisch's point was, and remains, an important one: some things that have been thought of as personal problems are in fact political. Calling them personal was a way for those with other interests to refuse to take the political problem seriously. Sometimes it's true, then, that 'the personal is political'. But it is important to note that what this slogan means is that *some things we thought were merely personal issues are in fact political issues*. What I thought was a problem with *my husband* is really a problem with *men*, or the ways that men and women are permitted to relate to each other in our current social and cultural context. The slogan doesn't mean *everything we thought was personal is in fact political*, which would mean *everything is political* – that there is no personal/political distinction at all. Of course there is; your sister has no filter, and for this reason you don't like to attend family dinners. That is not a political problem.

The collapse of the distinction between the personal and the political in at least some people's minds (we can argue about how widespread it is) has entailed the collapse of the distinction between the *moral* and the political, too. Where we might once have said, 'whether I attend the PETA demonstration against fur is political, but my own decision about what to eat for dinner is moral', we now tend to roll the two together, and see individual consumption decisions *as political*. Where we might once have been inclined to say that a man cheating on his wife was a matter of his moral failure – a lack of sexual self-restraint – some of us now appear inclined to talk about the evolutionary explanations of men 'spreading their seed' and the environmental (including institutional) conditions that now do or don't keep this inherited impulse in check.

In the politicizing of everything, we risk both undermining the moral and exaggerating the political: if he cheats because he's just an ape, really, and we're not currently doing a good enough job of civilizing the apes, then that's not his fault – it's *society*'s fault! And merely by choosing not to eat meat, a person has done something political, made a political contribution, even if no one knows or cares what they eat.[8] The collapse may also have other – compatible – explanations, including the rise of the idea that everything is ultimately about power (or that everything is ultimately discourse, and she who controls the discourse controls the world). If there's just one currency – power – and everyone's paying in it, it doesn't make sense to insist upon distinct domains governed by different standards, such as the moral and the political might otherwise be.

For the rest of this chapter, we will *accept* that there is no personal/political or moral/political distinction. (Many people today roll all these things together, which is likely to explain why they are strongly opposed to certain types of working together. We need to follow their lead in collapsing the relevant distinctions in order to be charitable about their reasons.) So any moral reasons you could have not to work with someone *are* reasons not to work with someone in pursuit of shared political goals. In fact, it's not just 'someone', it's also 'something': any moral reasons you could have not to work with informal and formal groups of individuals, companies and corporations, governments, non-governmental organizations and so on are also reasons not to work with those entities in pursuit of shared political goals.

Here are some things that people might have in mind when they object to 'working with' those they consider for some reason objectionable (I'll gloss this for now as those people being bad, having bad beliefs or having behaved badly):

- It rewards bad people with camaraderie, civility and the possibility of friendship and/or romance.
- It signals the acceptance of bad behaviour or agreement with bad beliefs.
- It risks incurring reciprocal obligations to do bad things.
- It misuses authority or credibility and thereby misleads people.
- It sacrifices integrity (creating 'dirty hands').

The first idea, that working with bad people rewards them with camaraderie, civility and the possibility of friendship and/or romance, relates to the social goods that are a normal part of working together, rather than the fact of working together itself. Suppose we all sign up for a day of picking up rubbish from the local beach, and throughout the day there are various interpersonal interactions: conversations, jokes, the discovering of commonalities and shared experiences, recommendations for podcasts and movies, whatever. We might think of these in moralized terms as 'rewards' that not everyone is due; only good people deserve to have others to talk to, laugh with, relate to, get recommendations from. Perhaps the very worst people are not due even civility: perhaps we ought to be especially awful to them, or indeed ostracize and exclude them. Working with bad people is wrong *because* it passes along goods that the bad person is not entitled to.[9] The second idea, 'Accepting bad behaviour or agreeing with bad beliefs', relates to what working together may entail or be assumed to entail. Say your business partner is abusive towards your employees and yet you continue to work with her. It may be that this is because you don't see her behaviour as a problem, or perhaps you see it as a problem but have your own private reasons to keep working together, which you don't communicate – so you are *assumed to* accept her behaviour.

There are two philosophy papers that take up these issues in the context of the nearby issue of being *friends with* bad people. This is not quite our issue because working with someone need not, and often will not, mean being friends with them (although it may create the possibility of friendship, and perhaps there are some cases in which even creating this possibility is wrong). But some of the reasons not to be friends with bad people might apply to working with bad people, so for that reason they're worth considering.

Jessica Isserow argues that those who have bad people as friends are morally complacent because we choose our friends, and our choice of friends should be '*responsive to* another's virtues and vices . . . there are certain vices of which [one] could not possibly be forgiving . . . there are particular moral flaws which no wholly decent person could tolerate'.[10] Naturally we might wonder what kinds of things count as vices of this kind. Isserow says she is interested in moral vices 'that we tend to regard as especially serious – cruelty, strong disregard for the welfare of others, callousness, and the like',[11] and not 'less serious moral vices such as rudeness and miserliness', or 'faults of character' like 'ineptitude and cowardice'.[12]

Her main example is racism: we can forgive a failure to recycle but not 'rampant racism'.[13] Isserow thinks that discounting rampant racism shows that the person in question does not care about the values that support anti-racism (like equality), or about the victims of racism.[14] There is a certain kind of selfishness here, a not caring about how a friend hurts *others* so long as they do not hurt *you*. And there's a certain kind of expressive failure, not being sympathetic with the victims of the person's vices nor being appropriately angry on their behalf.[15]

It is somewhat strange that *racism* is the main example of a bad person who we might not want to be friends with when the universe of especially serious moral vice is so kaleidoscopic. It might say more about the political orientation of the author and the current influence of identity politics that it is racism (which at its weakest might be nothing more than the expression of a bad attitude without *any* causal effects on anyone) rather than, say, having been convicted of child abuse, rape, domestic violence or murder; or being convicted of torture, human trafficking or terrorism. Isserow's considerations apply quite well to the question of Prince Andrew's friendship with Jeffrey Epstein[16]; less well, I think, to whether two mates from the construction site should keep getting beers together because one has questionable opinions about immigrants. Let's replace racism with sexual exploitation as a clear example of a bad person that there is a question about working with (and especially salient for who *feminists* should work with).

Can the considerations that Isserow mobilizes to argue against *being friends with* bad people be applied straightforwardly to *working with* bad people? One complication comes with the claim that we choose our friends. Whether this is true of our friends, it is often *not* true of those we work with. A company hires its employees; the employees are stuck with each other. A university admits its students; the students are stuck with each other. The charity recruits its volunteers; the club selects its members; the craft meet-ups advertise and accept all comers. There may be limited voluntarism within these limits, for example, there is a certain latitude for manoeuvring into different teams at work, or different small groups in university tutorials. One can always quit the club, quit volunteering for the charity, quit going to the craft meet-ups. But for a lot of the occasions where we end up working with other people, we are pushed together by circumstance (and that is part of what makes life interesting), *not* choosing who to interact with. In most cases, we'll be in complete ignorance of the other person's virtues and vices and may only come to learn about them much later. If we do not choose in the first place, then it can't be that we must be responsive to the individual's virtues and vices when we choose.

The part of the view that does apply is that *if and when* we come to know about a workmate's serious moral vice – serious like sexual exploitation – and we have some control over whether we choose to work with them or not and choose not to exercise it, then, and only then, might we be said to be displaying moral complacency and expressing a kind of indifference towards the victims of that person's moral crimes.

Cathy Mason also takes up the question of friendship with bad people, arguing that there are some loving relationships where it is permissible to be in them with bad people, and others where it is not – friendship being one of the latter. She notes that we think it appropriate for parents and mentors to maintain their relationships with children and mentees respectively, even when the children and mentees are bad people.[17] Mason thinks that friendship involves *'taking one's friends seriously'*,[18] meaning, taking their beliefs or attitudes to be at least prima facie valuable.[19] If your friend loves opera, then you should be open-minded about the value of opera, even when you have previously disliked it.[20] The same goes for matters in the political arena: 'if a friend has firm political convictions that matter a lot to them, their conviction itself gives one reason to take that political position seriously, and to need a reason to reject it.'[21] But 'since some moral views and perspectives should not be taken seriously or considered as options, friendship with bad people is itself morally bad in that respect'.[22] We *shouldn't* be open to, or give serious consideration to, 'deeply immoral views and attitudes'.[23] This gets to the matter of working together implying acceptance of, or agreement with, bad beliefs.

Again, we need to know what kinds of moral views and perspectives Mason has in mind and, again, racism is the go-to: 'I am thinking about friendships with individuals who have *serious* moral deficiencies, not merely minor flaws – unrepentant racists and misogynists, for example, rather than those whose humour may sometimes err towards the uncomfortable.'[24] Mason says that 'matters on which there is genuine and sincere moral disagreement' are excluded, but then goes on to say, 'The very willingness even to question women's moral status seems like a kind of misogyny.'[25] That is, being friends with a misogynist means being open to the idea that there's something to misogyny, and that itself is *a kind of* misogyny. Being friends with bad people causes you to take morally repugnant views seriously, which you should not do.

Again, this point would have been more effective with a more credible example. While there certainly are plenty of outright misogynists, there are also many people engaged in *genuine and sincere moral disagreement* about the extent of sex differences. What looks to a 'sameness' feminist like misogyny looks to a 'difference' feminist like reality. Those committed to sameness will deny there is genuine and sincere moral disagreement, while those committed to difference will insist that there is. Is the alleged misogynist a bad person, and so the kind of person who should have no friends, or not? Are we really prepared to say that all the difference feminists *should have no friends*? (I am a sameness feminist, and I find this conclusion absurd.)

This reveals a more general problem that gets to the heart of matters at stake in this book. Of course, if we could all agree about who was 'bad', then we could agree about who we shouldn't work with. But given that we disagree about who is 'bad', and either political side goes about calling the other one bad, is there anything more principled – or objective – that can be said? This is not a retreat into moral nihilism: there are some things that are obviously morally bad, like sex trafficking or torturing people for not-massively-consequential reasons. But *a lot* of what gets treated as morally obvious is not, and is in fact a matter of reasonable disagreement. The

82 Reasons to Not 'Work With'

hard work of making moral arguments is avoided by a kind of table-thumping about moral matters.

Perhaps we can get a more principled and objective approach out of thinking not about who we should and shouldn't be friends with but about when certain negative moral emotions are justified. If the standards of application are clear enough *for* expressing these emotions at targets, then we'll be able to *check* whether they apply in the case of people working together on a specific project, including feminists working with individuals or groups from/of 'team red' on a specific project like abortion rights or the prohibition of child medical transition. With this in mind, let's turn to some recent work on what is perhaps the most *severe* of the negative moral emotions, namely contempt.

Macalester Bell defends the possibility of an individual's feeling or expression of contempt being a moral or political accomplishment. She's specifically interested in the idea that women feeling or expressing contempt against men 'within a context of male domination' is a *feminist* accomplishment.[26] She understands contempt to have the following 'four distinguishing features':

- '[C]ontempt is a response to a perceived *failure to meet an interpersonal standard*'.[27]
- 'It is . . . a particular way of *regarding* or *attending* to the object of contempt [that] has an unpleasant affective element.'[28]
- '[C]ontempt has an important *comparative* element. . . . [It] requires apprehending the bad qualities of someone "as they really are", while simultaneously making a comparison between this person and ourselves'.[29]
- 'A final characteristic of contempt is the psychological withdrawal or distance one typically feels regarding the object of one's contempt. . . . This psychological distancing is a way of expressing one's nonidentification with the object of one's

contempt and it precludes sympathetic identification with the object of contempt.'[30]

Importantly, Bell notes that such contempt is *justified* only when the target really does fail to achieve the interpersonal standard and when the standard is itself justified. These are objective-sounding criteria: there's a fact of the matter both about what our interpersonal standards are and about whether a particular individual has in fact fallen well short of meeting them. Her main example comes from the 1963 film *Contempt*, in which a husband 'appears to be willing to trade the possibility of [his wife's] sexual services in return for [his own] professional success'.[31] The wife, Camille, in the film becomes increasingly contemptuous towards her husband; Bell 'use[s] the example of Camille's contempt to urge a distinctly feminist defence of the emotion'.[32]

Her strategy in the paper is to consider feminist defences of other moral emotions, including anger and bitterness, in order to extract a range of reasons *why* those emotions are feminist achievements, and then to argue that those same reasons apply in the case of contempt. Those reasons are that negative emotions can be an act of insubordination, itself a way of maintaining self-respect; can lead to new forms of knowledge; can be a way of bearing witness to injustice; and can be motivating in a way that leads to social change.[33]

Camille's contempt for her husband in the film is a form of emotional insubordination; 'she takes herself to be *morally* superior to [the husband] Paul. This claim of superiority constitutes an act of insubordination in contexts in which women are generally regarded as inferior to men.'[34] And in the film, the husband in fact responds to Camille's contempt as a superior would to the insubordination of an inferior. Bell thinks the very feeling of contempt by women may give women knowledge: 'a woman's feelings of contempt for sexist men and institutions give women knowledge about their oppression lacking to those who are not oppressed.'[35] Observation of whether women's contempt is given uptake can also provide knowledge about women's social standing, for example when it is 'not intelligible or viable'.[36] Bell gives an example involving the very narrow range of contexts (in low-brow jokes and on greeting cards) in which women's contemptuous comments about men get uptake – and even then possibly only by other women.[37] Camille's contempt for her husband in the film was not only an act of emotional subordination, but also something that 'allow[ed] her to bear witness to Paul's character deficit'.[38] Finally, because contempt leads to disengagement, it can be motivating when distancing is an effective response, for example in motivating Camille to end her marriage to Paul. It can also lead to the target of contempt considering whether they endorse the interpersonal standard they're being held to and 'have in fact failed to live up to standards that we care about'.[39] This may lead to a transformation of the target (although of course if they reject the standard it will not). Just as Marilyn Frye talked about women's anger leading to physical separation from men, Bell suggests that contempt may lead to 'women psychologically distancing themselves from sexist men and male-dominated institutions'.[40]

Does this get us closer to what we need? Bell's focus is on women, but that seems to be *because* she takes women to be oppressed: 'women are members of an oppressed group.'[41] She writes 'Those who are contemptuous of their oppressors recognize that systems of oppression preclude relationships of mutual respect and engagement between oppressors and oppressed.'[42] So we should be able to generalize the case for contempt at least to other oppressed groups. The problem, of course, is that neither *the left* nor *the right* is an oppressed group. ('Tribe left' does tend to present itself as the only one that represents the interests of oppressed groups, but that is not the same thing.) And neither, even, is any subgroup therein, like 'the far left' (whatever exactly that term refers to) or 'the religious right'.

There may be individuals on either side who plausibly stand in oppressor–oppressed relations, for example, conservative men and progressive women (oppressor–oppressed on the axis of sex/gender), or white conservatives and Black progressives (oppressor–oppressed on the axis of race). But that doesn't get us to *the whole left* counting as oppressed, and therefore of being justified in the feeling or expression of contempt towards the right (and because of contempt for the right, towards anyone of/affiliated with the right). What goes for women in a male-dominated context simply does not go for those from one place on a political spectrum towards those on another. Or not in virtue of their politics, at least.

What if we forget about the oppressor–oppressed relation and focus on the interpersonal standards alone? Bell says that contempt is a response to the perceived failure of another to meet some interpersonal standard. In order not to beg any questions, we can't simply insist that the correct interpersonal standard is 'being left wing'. If it was, then it's an easy win: everyone right-wing has failed to meet the interpersonal standard of being left wing, and contempt is justified. Contempt means distancing, and a pleasing sense of oneself as morally superior – which is explanatory of what we actually see. On Bell's understanding of contempt, there is, plausibly, political contempt coming from each side towards the other; the question is only whether it is *justified* in her sense. To be justified there must actually be a standard, and the targeted individuals must actually fail to meet it.

If there are plausible ways to fill in the interpersonal standard, such that there really is *one* such standard (and not one for 'team left' and another for 'team right'), then this will be a promising way to approach the question of justified contempt, and the refusal to work together that is a natural outcome of the distancing that contempt involves. Some ways to fill in this standard can be generated by the candidate distinctions between left and right mentioned in chapter 4. Suppose our interpersonal standard is 'protect the vulnerable', and it is claimed that the left upholds that standard through generous social welfare provisions while the right does not because of its cuts to social welfare programmes. Then *for* failing to meet the interpersonal standard, contempt *towards the right* is justified. The problem – and Lewis and Lewis's reason for rejecting all such proposed distinctions – is that this standard is specified too broadly to adequately distinguish left from right. The right will say it's protecting the vulnerable by opposing abortion and that it's the left who is failing to meet that interpersonal standard. Again, this is not a plea for moral nihilism or relativism; it's a plea for more generosity in what counts as a reasonable disagreement (on which, more on pp. 91–5).[43]

Before we move on to other moral reasons not to work together, let me make a few more general points relating to the two ideas considered in this section. We could adapt a more general version of Isserow's argument, and say it is wrong to *associate with* (not only be friends with) bad people, for the same reasons that she gives. Working with people is a way of associating with them so it's wrong to work with bad people.[44] But this can't be right. I've already said that a lot of working together is unavoidable, e.g., that which happens in the course of paid employment. (Or if not strictly unavoidable, the costs of not working with bad people are too high for there to be any general injunction against it.) It also seems clear that sometimes working with bad people is a *good thing*, revealing positive character traits, such as when Daryl Davis befriended hundreds of Ku Klux Klan members and caused them to leave the Klan,[45] or when Shirley Chisholm (the first Black woman elected to the United States Congress) visited her political opponent George Wallace – 'perhaps the single most famous supporter of racial segregation in modern history' – in hospital.[46]

We could also insist that working together always implies condoning the other's behaviour or views. It is wrong to condone bad behaviour or views, so it is wrong to work with people who do it/have them. But, again, this can't be right. How well known is the bad behaviour? How strong an association between the behaviour and the person is there? What is it that you're working together *to do*? (This may help to establish which of their beliefs or behaviours are even *relevant*.) How does the public/private distinction feature – is there a difference between continuing to work with your business partner when she is abusive towards your employees and continuing to work with her when she serially cheats on her boyfriends? What if you make clear you disapprove of the specific bad behaviour, or you do something about it (like introducing a complaints pathway and remedies for the employees who experienced her abusive behaviour or insisting your business partner takes an anger management course), *then* can you keep working together? And when do you actually *need* to make such disapproval clear, when are you merely virtue signalling (and so doing something self-aggrandizing) or bowing to political pressure (and so being cowardly), rather than acting to address reasonable concerns?

One final idea that might be worth considering is the idea of disassociation (refusal to work with) as futile resistance.[47] In her 1988 book *Lesbian Ethics*, Sarah Lucia Hoagland articulated an idea of agency under oppression. Here's her commentary some four years later:

> In addition to an obsession with rules and principles, fraternal agency focuses on free will, and we are encouraged to think that to be moral agents we must have free will. Thus, when in understanding ourselves as oppressed we find we don't have free will, we are tempted to think we can't be moral agents and consequently to think of ourselves merely as victims. Lesbians exist within a context of oppression. Any moral or political theory useful to anyone under oppression must not convince

88 Reasons to Not 'Work With'

us that either we must be in complete control or we are total
victims. While we don't control situations, we do affect them.
It is crucial to understand ourselves not as mere victims but as
participants who are oppressed.[48]

'Fraternal agency' here refers to the background idea that
'Anglo-European ethics' is inadequate,[49] at least partly because
it has been so male dominated and male centred.

If I can be permitted a little philosophical pedantry,
Hoagland's reference to 'free will' is mistaken because the free-
will debate is not about whether specific individual actions are
free but about whether freedom of choice is possible within
a deterministic universe. It is about an entailment from fun-
damental physics to morality, not about whether coercion,
control, oppression or severely constrained option sets under-
mine an individual's freedom when it comes to her choices (or
what she consents to). But her point is clear enough: a dominant way of thinking tells us we are either agents or victims,
that if we are oppressed we are victims and so not agents, that
if we are agents then we are not victims and so not oppressed.[50]
She was writing about lesbians (and lesbian separatist communities) at a time when lesbians were oppressed. And her
point was we are *both* oppressed and have agency. Agency is
not limited to full control of a situation. She gave the following
delightful example, which illustrates the idea of agency under
oppression and gives us an example of futile resistance ('futile'
as to getting the ideal outcome):

I was fired, essentially, from two jobs before I received tenure
(after a dogfight) at my present university. I chose to bring a
discrimination suit against the second one (together with the
other woman in the department who was also dumped). I chose
to bring that suit not because I thought I was going to get my
job back, and I did not, and not because I thought I was going to
get financial compensation and I did not, but because I had to

say, 'Fuck you, you will not go on as if I never existed; you may fire me, but I'm going to cause you a lot of trouble', and I did.[51]

We can affect situations even when we don't control them; Hoagland affected the institution that discriminated against her, even when she could not control the outcome of being reinstated or being compensated. If we apply this idea to the claim that feminists should not work with the right, it gives us a sort of rationale. Those who refuse to work with the right cannot control *that* there is a 'team right'; perhaps they very much wish there wasn't. They can't control the right finding allies in feminists other than themselves; perhaps they constantly post inefficacious tweets, imploring other feminists not to work with the right, that get few views and even fewer likes. All they have control over is what *they* do, so they loudly refuse to work with the right, disassociate *themselves* from the right, repudiate and denounce the right, and so on. They exercise agency but not full control. What they do may be entirely futile measured against the goal of bringing it about that there is no right, or that feminists do not work with the right. Still, they are doing *something*; they are 'going down fighting'.

The application is not perfectly straightforward because, as came up in discussing Bell's case for morally justified contempt, the relation between feminists who refuse to work with the right and the right (and between feminists who refuse to work with the right and feminists who are happy to work with the right) is not one of *oppression*. If Hoagland's intervention on the victim/agency dichotomy depends on there being an actual victim, then 'team left' feminists are not candidates for exercising agency under oppression. (If they are not oppressed in the first place, they can't be exercising agency under oppression.) There is also the complication that 'team left' feminists sometimes perform these behaviours in contexts in which the left is dominant, like the university, or in states with secure 'team left' governments (so, if we had to describe things in oppressor/oppressed terms, the left would be the oppressor, not the oppressed). Still, the idea might be explanatory. If those feminists think of the grand struggle between left and right *as* the grand struggle between good and evil, then it will be incomprehensible to them that *they, the left*, could be *the oppressor*, and so, no matter the context, their 'fight' against the right, futile or not, will appear to them as the fight against evil, the fight from the side of the oppressed.[52]

There are a number of other moral reasons that might be offered against working with bad people. In the course of working together, the bad person may help you out in ways that mean you come to have obligations of reciprocity to them. They may then 'cash in' on those obligations in a way that pushes you towards doing things you consider morally bad. There is a corporate/institutional version of this: if you accept an in-kind contribution, such as a venue or funding, from a group with bad views, you set yourself up for reciprocal obligations to that group that you may consider distasteful. If you have more authority or credibility than the bad person, then merely by working together you may transfer some of your authority or credibility to them by signalling that *this is a person I take seriously, this is a person I am happy to be publicly associated with, this is a person I have esteem for.* (Here, similarly, there is a corporate/institutional version.) Working together with a bad person may compromise your integrity: say you are a struggling actor who does not approve of meat eaters and tries to stay away from them as much as possible; but then you get an exciting offer to feature in a film with a co-star who not only eats meat but likes to share photos of herself eating steak on social media to provoke the vegans. If you take the role, you compromise your integrity and make yourself a hypocrite.

It's not as though these reasons *never* apply. Certainly, we can incur reciprocal obligations and feel we have little choice in fulfilling them when the other party decides it's time to cash in. Certainly, transfer of authority or credibility is possible. And certainly, there are instances in which people clearly compromise their integrity. The question for us is whether it's remotely plausible that *working with* someone 'bad' on a shared project does any or all of these things. We can accept help in ways that make it clear we're not accepting any strings attached. We can say 'no' when asked to do things we're not comfortable with, even if we 'owe someone one'. Sometimes working together is no more and no less than a surprising alliance – it doesn't mean either party's authority or credibility, if they have any, is being transferred to the other. It's altogether too easy to imagine that the liked party has authority and credibility and that's being transferred to the disliked party. But we shouldn't confuse our likes and dislikes for what is objectively the case. (Why, when the question is feminists working with 'the right', is the assumption always that *we* transfer our authority or credibility to *them*, rather than the other way around? Couldn't it be that they are the ones lending authority and credibility to us, and taking us to new audiences? Or couldn't it be both, in equal measure – a mutually beneficial alliance?) Finally, not everything we disapprove of is a matter of our integrity. We should not compromise on what is important to us (unless greatly more important interests are at stake), but it is perfectly possible to not compromise on that *and* still work together with people we disagree with or even dislike.

We have a problem: moralized mistreatment of *bad people* appears to be sometimes justified, but we don't know who the *bad people* are. Each political team thinks it's the other one. Is there anything we can say that sidesteps this problem and uses a more objective procedure? One way to think about interpersonal standards that doesn't beg any questions in this way is to set a threshold level of social agreement, and then use survey data that take the attitudes of the population as they are to check thresholds. Anything outside the threshold is unreasonable, and is therefore justified grounds for moralized mistreatment; anything inside the threshold is reasonable, so is *unjustified* grounds for moralized mistreatment. It doesn't matter whether the entire population is prejudiced (and are therefore 'bad people' in the view of some outsiders). All that matters is what they agree upon versus what they are divided over. Obviously, we don't want to set the threshold at a point that allows the country to be more or less evenly divided on an issue because that would only result in two teams directing moralized mistreatment at each other, which is no improvement on the political polarization we already have. So 50% won't do as a threshold.

Suppose we set the threshold at 66.66%, to capture a two-thirds majority. In 2017, it was announced that 61.6% of Australian voters supported same-sex marriage. Support differed state by state, with the lowest support in New South Wales (which contains the city of Sydney) at 58%, and the highest support in the Australian Capital Territory (ACT) (which contains the Federal Parliament) at 74%. *Only* the ACT had over 66.66%. The range for the other six states was 58–65% (the highest percentage in this range being Victoria, which contains the city of Melbourne).[53] So even though the vote returned by the referendum was sufficient for Australia to introduce gay marriage, it would *not* count as a sufficient result to justify contempt towards those who disagreed and voted against it, if we used the two-thirds majority threshold. The Pew Research Center reported in May 2024 that nearly two years after the overturning of *Roe v. Wade*, 'a majority of Americans continue to express support for abortion access'.[54] Of Americans, 63% said abortion should be legal in all or most cases (up from 60% in 1995), and 36% said it should be illegal in all or most cases (down from 38% in 1995). Again, 63% is less than our two-thirds threshold, so would make abortion a reasonable disagreement, inappropriate for moralized mistreatment, not an unreasonable one. Expressing contempt for people with different views about legal abortion (in whichever direction) would not be justified.

There are some obvious problems with this approach. First of all, it quite deliberately cannot distinguish between *progressive disagreement* and *regressive disagreement*. Consider a highly religious society with strong gender roles, in which some feminists emerge, contesting that this is the natural order of things and arguing for greater equality between the sexes. But because many people sincerely believe in the religion that promulgates those roles, many people see the feminists as crazy/mad/deluded. There are few converts to their cause. Say the percentage of feminists in the population never gets above 5%. Compare this against the highly secular society in which there is a lot of sexual promiscuity and in which some 'sexual reactionaries' appear, arguing for a return to past ideals of sex within committed loving relationships only, ideally marriages. And say the same thing happens to these dissidents – against the prevailing ideology, they look crazy/mad/deluded, there are few converts to their cause and their numbers never rise above 5% of the population. Don't we want to distinguish these two cases, and say the first is *progressive disagreement* and so the feminists should not be the targets of contempt, while the second is a *regressive disagreement* and so the sexual reactionaries should (or may) be the targets of contempt? And if so, doesn't this take us away from the neutral procedure, which allows them both to be targets of contempt, and pulls us back towards the 'bad people' procedure, in which we can be confident about contempt being justified, but stymied at the question of who its appropriate targets actually are?

I think we can answer this question with a 'no'. The dissidents, whether they are progressive or regressive, must make their case and win over the public.[55] This may be a long, hard battle, and they may well lose it. That is just what it is to live in a liberal democracy. *While* they are below the threshold, their disagreement is not yet reasonable, and they may be the

94 Reasons to Not 'Work With'

targets of moralized mistreatment. If we want to avoid this conclusion, we should say that *no one* is an appropriate target of moralized mistreatment. (To me, that is the most tempting solution, and I think the more strategic one.)

Another problem with this approach is that it may seem to fetishize agreement, when we know that conformism and tribalism play a huge role in what people agree *about*. If we thought that social consensus (at two-thirds or above) *meant* the truth had been discovered, then we'd be more justified in approaching agreement in this way, but what about when we know there's no such correlation? Again, I don't think this is such a serious objection. The threshold doesn't depend on what the majority achieves, it just depends on there being a majority. It's a way of dividing what is still a 'live issue' for the society from what is more or less settled.

A third problem is not with the threshold per se but with setting it at 66.66%: this gets things precisely the wrong way around. The *more* people there are who disagree about a topic, the *safer* it is to let contempt be directed at them. The teams are evenly matched, so no one's going to lose job opportunities and social relationships for being on one team or the other. The more that some group is a minority, the more vulnerable they are – so we should be concerned to protect *both* the feminists and the sexual reactionaries in the cases above. There's something to this concern, although it's not quite true that the closer to 50:50 the division, the more protected people are because it will probably be that one team or the other will dominate across different institutions, as we in fact see with 'team left' and universities. In the contexts where one team dominates, those from the other team may well lose job opportunities and social relationships. If I'm asked which I'd prefer, a society divided roughly into halves and in which each side is contemptuous towards the other, or a society divided into a large majority and a small minority in which the majority and the minority are contemptuous towards each other,

I'd say the former *because* I'd be worried that the asymmetry in social power between the majority and the minority in the latter would lead to worse outcomes for the minority-group members. But if I got to choose between a society without contempt for moral and political disagreements and a society with contempt, I'd certainly choose the former. There are better ways to deal with disagreement.

Is it feasible that we can allow moralized *social* mistreatment while protecting against moralized *legal* mistreatment? That is, can we protect people in the spheres of life where it matters, like the workplace, while allowing contempt to *otherwise* run wild? That is, after all, what we appear to be trying to do in countries that have workplace protections extending to philosophical and political beliefs (some versions of which exist in the United Kingdom and Australia, at least). I'm sceptical, from my experience inside the university, that this really works. It would appear to work on paper much better than it works in practice. If it really worked in practice, wouldn't we expect universities to have *more faculty from 'team right'*? Policies that protect the beliefs of those who are *already employees* cannot protect those applying to become employees.

Earlier in this chapter, I noted that the embrace of the idea that 'the personal is political' (along with other factors, potentially) has led to a collapse of a personal/political or moral/political distinction. In order to be charitable to the rationales for not working with others, we have been proceeding without those distinctions. But questions about what the best interpersonal response is to particular individuals known to have certain views that we ourselves, or others, find (or claim to find) morally repugnant[56] are *not the same* as questions about acceptable strategic alliances, and about the limits, if there are any, to politically non-partisan or 'hands across the aisle' coalitions.

Suppose that someone reveals themselves to have horrible views – say, they are deeply anti-Semitic. One question we can ask is, What is the right way to respond to this person's expression of those views? Perhaps we have visceral emotional responses to expressions of hatred like this, so any way that we respond is excused (we couldn't have done any differently). When we don't, we might think about what an appropriate response would be (e.g., voicing clear disagreement), and what kind of response would be most likely to get the ultimate outcome we seek. If we want there to be less anti-Semitism in the world, then simply expressing repugnance may not be the best way to respond. We might consult the psychology literature to find out what 'calling out', shaming, denouncing, social ostracism and so on do to the people who are called out, shamed, denounced, ostracized. Does it work, resulting in a change in their attitudes, or does it further radicalize and entrench their views because they feel misunderstood, caricatured, condescended to? – because if there is no relationship left to preserve, there can be no reason to work to preserve it?

The ideas surveyed in this chapter speak mostly to this set of questions. But the claim I'm addressing in this book relates to a second set of questions, namely, whether and when feminists should work together with other groups in pursuit of shared ends. Feminism is a political project, not a personal project. It is collective, not individual. We're not asking about what individuals who happen to be feminists should do *morally*, we're asking about what feminists as feminists should do *politically*. Suppose the University of Melbourne had a student free-speech society, made up mostly of libertarian students. Should I, as a radical feminist, partner with that society in order to put on an event to platform a frequently de-platformed feminist speaker? We have shared ends in the protection of feminist speech, they because they care about *free* speech and I because I care about *feminist* speech. That shared end coexists alongside many disagreements in other areas – suppose they are opposed to the government prohibition of prostitution and pornography (as libertarians tend to be), while I am in favour of it. Still, we might set that disagreement aside for the purpose of this event. The question will be whether, for each of us, we should. We can roughly draw this distinction between interpersonal response and strategic collaboration as the distinction between *the moral* and *the political*. This distinction has been collapsed or occluded in the way that some progressives do (or claim to do) politics today. It's time to reinstate it.

Here's Carl Schmitt in his 1932 book, *The Concept of the Political*:

> The political must therefore rest on its own ultimate distinctions, to which all action with a specifically political meaning can be traced. Let us assume that in the realm of morality the final distinctions are between good and evil, in aesthetics beautiful and ugly, in economics profitable and unprofitable. The question then is whether there is also a special distinction which can serve as a simple criterion of the political and of what it consists. ... The specific political distinction to which political actions and motives can be reduced is that between friend and enemy.[57]

Where I have been using 'good' and 'bad' in talking about morality, Schmitt uses 'good' and 'evil'. That good and evil is the final distinction of morality is self-explanatory, but what does Schmitt mean when he says that 'friend and enemy' is the final distinction of politics? These words are not being used in their ordinary way. (It is especially important to acknowledge this, given that we have been talking in this chapter about whether there are reasons not to be friends with bad people, and that is an ordinary sense of 'friends'.) It is not that questions about individuals are moral questions and questions about groups are political questions. We could ask the moral question in both cases: is this individual evil, is this group evil, and if so, is spending time with them (or in them) likely to make *me* evil – or more likely to make *them* good? We can also ask the political question in both cases: is this individual my enemy, is this group my enemy, and, if they're not, indeed, they could be my friend (in Schmitt's sense), what reason could there be not to work with them?

Schmitt says that, 'The distinction of friend and enemy denotes the utmost degree of intensity of a union or separation, of an association or dissociation.'[58] And he goes on: 'Only the actual participants can correctly recognize, understand, and judge the concrete situation and settle the extreme case of conflict. Each participant is in a position to judge whether the adversary *intends to negate his opponent's way of life and therefore must be repulsed or fought in order to preserve one's own form of existence.*'[59]

The 'enemy', then, is a threat to our 'way of life', who we must fight in order to protect that way of life. This makes the most sense at the level of the nation-state, when we are thinking about the real prospect of a war or invasion, and whether to resist it. But it is not restricted to relations between states; the friend/enemy relation can also hold between smaller groups of people. (I am not sure whether Schmitt thinks it can hold between individuals.)

The *different* distinctions of morality and politics make clear that one can be evil while being a friend, and good while being an enemy.[60] Our judgement as to a group's or individual's *moral* status does not entail or even imply a judgement as to its or their *political* status. Its political status can only be determined relative to our own way of life. Let me make this point by returning to the most extreme example from the Preface, the members of the white supremacist National Socialist Network who counter-protested a protest of the Let Women Speak event in Melbourne in 2023. It is *conceptually possible*, meaning it is not ruled out in principle, that these men could have been both 'evil' and 'friends' to the gender-critical feminists and others who were on the women's side of the conflict between women's rights and trans rights being addressed at the Let Women Speak event. In case this strikes you as an incredible claim, consider that the men (at the time, distinguishable only as a small group of white males dressed in black)[61] were both law abiding[62] and posed no physical threat to the Let Women Speak attendees – in striking contrast to the protesters (socialists and trans activists) who were screaming threats and straining to break through police lines. Indeed, considering the events carefully in retrospect, there is some reason to think their presence *prevented* violence against the Let Women Speak attendees by counter-protesters.[63] (Of course, that they represented no immediate physical threat to the Let Women Speak attendees is not sufficient to establish that there's no conflict between the 'way of life' of the two groups, but the National Socialist Network do not have a public policy/position statement online, so it is harder to assess that issue, at least without spending many hours trawling through their videos in order to try to cobble some version of their ideology together.)

The National Workers Alliance, or Matt Trihey as an alleged 'fascist'[64] involved in some way with the 2024 Women Will Speak event in Melbourne, could similarly have been both 'evil' and a 'friend'. So too for the Heritage Foundation in 2019 and everyone else at the London rally against two-tier policing in 2024 (or just Tommy Robinson, the organizer). This is not to declare that all of these people or organizations are in fact morally evil, it is merely to make the point that *even if they are*, that does not rule out their being 'friends' to feminists politically. Any combination of the moral and the political – good/ friend, bad/friend, good/enemy, bad/enemy – is possible. To figure out *whether* any of these groups were in fact 'friends' or 'enemies', we would need to work through what they stand for, and how that relates to the understanding of women's equality, self-determination, liberation or interests that each type of feminist has. We'll do exactly that for one candidate 'friend' of at least one type of feminist in chapter 6.

100   Reasons to Not 'Work With'

Is drawing the moral/political distinction in terms of Schmitt's friend/enemy bringing a cannon to a knife fight? After all, Schmitt is careful to distinguish the relation of infighting factions from groups having friend/enemy status. Not only the possible political alliances but also the 'team left' feminist backlash *against* those possible alliances all happen within a liberal state. So why not say *we're all friends*, and none of this is 'the political' in Schmitt's sense? I've said already that the friend/enemy distinction is not limited to relations between states. The issue for us to work out is what sorts of disagreements between groups within states *count as* threats to our group's 'way of life', repulsion of which is necessary in order to preserve our group's 'form of existence'. We have to be careful with concept creep here – some groups prominent in contemporary identity politics routinely invoke threats to their 'existence' when they mean threats to their *identity*. Identity might, but need not, rise to the level of a 'way of life' or 'form of existence' – it depends on how important it is, and whether it can coexist in harmony with others with *different* ways of life and forms of existence. A paradigm case here is religious pluralism: as strongly as people feel about the religious doctrine they adhere to, they are also capable, within liberal democracies, of not seeing others having different religions, or no religion, as a threat to *their* religious practice. Even when the stakes are high, we are generally able to 'live and let live'.

This is actually helpful for thinking about the question of male-supremacist feminists that posed a challenge to some of our initial definitions in chapter 1. Women who want to belong to a male-headed traditional family can realize their desires compatible with other women not belonging to such families. Male-supremacist women can *lament* other women's choices to not have families or to have different family arrangements, just as a religious person might lament the atheists or those of other faiths. But as long as those others' choices do not prevent your own, both your individual choices and your ability to form associations with others who share your beliefs, then they are *not* a threat. And if they are not a threat, then they are not the enemy in Schmitt's sense, and you need not 'fight' or 'repulse' them. Indeed, you could work with them in pursuit of shared ends: you could be friends. Schmitt's conception of the 'enemy' is *not* a cannon at a knife fight. Rather, it helps us to assess the seriousness of our disagreements, and to deploy moralized mistreatment[65] only where it is truly justified.

Let's return to Greta from chapter 3, who was engaged in the social targeting of a pro-life volunteer at a women's homelessness shelter. Greta's mistake was to conflate the moral and the political. *Again: there are no individual solutions to political problems.* Libby is not 'the enemy' of Greta; they have a moral disagreement, and it is a reasonable disagreement in both the ordinary sense and the social sense considered in terms of empirical thresholds introduced earlier. One issue is whether moralized mistreatment such as Greta's even works (given that voting is private and the numbers are so high that no one will know, together with the fact that moralized mistreatment can breed resentment); another is that such mistreatment is undesirable as an ordinary feature of life, whether inside or outside of the workplace. *Everyone* feels the stakes are high for the things they care about morally. But we all have an interest in living in a society without interpersonal mistreatment and contempt – or at least, reserving such negative treatment and emotions for the extreme cases where they are really justified. Contempt against sex traffickers, yes; contempt against those who think 'marriage' should be exclusively between a man and a woman, no.

Suppose that *what it is* to make a negative moral judgement is to feel strong negative emotions towards the object of the judgement and to disassociate from them. Does that show that there can be no moral/political distinction, where we behave in these ways only in the moral but not in the political domain? (Or only in the private sphere but not in the public sphere?) The *feelings* might be involuntary, and necessarily connected to a moral judgement, but the *expression* of those feelings surely is not. We can build strong norms and conventions against the expression of those feelings in the political domain/public sphere. Christians, for example, hold themselves to standards for interpersonal interaction that act to mask or block the expression of interpersonal contempt, or the desire to withdraw. Even when they disagree morally, they may be committed to treating the other with kindness, compassion and understanding.[66] Epistemic norms of humility may do the same thing, tempering the expression that may follow from certainty by adding just enough doubt to cause restraint.[67] So even if there will be contempt and other negative emotions, or a desire to withdraw or disassociate wherever there is moral judgement, that is not a reason to think that the expression of these feelings between those who disagree politically is unavoidable. Greta need not have treated Libby the way she did; we can cultivate norms to minimize the occasions on which such moralized mistreatment is considered acceptable.

Once we make a moral/political distinction, it becomes clear that there are a lot of people simply doing morality and calling it politics. If some person or group *really is our enemy*, then we must do whatever it takes to defeat them; working with a bad person will be the least of our issues.[68] And if some person or group is within the large and heterogeneous group labelled 'friend' (in Schmitt's sense), then we have no in-principle reason not to work together. What remains are merely strategic considerations about whether working with them is likely to help us to achieve our goals. I'll turn to those considerations in the final chapter.

6

Moving Forward with Non-Partisan Feminism

> Feminism is a political practice of fighting male supremacy on behalf of women as a class, including all the women you don't like, including all the women you don't want to be around, including all the women who used to be your best friends whom you don't want anything to do with any more. It doesn't matter who the individual women are.
>
> Andrea Dworkin, 1990 [1987]

> In reality, the status and treatment of women has certain regularities across time and space, making gender a group experience of inequality on the basis of sex.
>
> Catharine MacKinnon, 1991

Historically, 'radical' men told 'radical' women that other issues were more important than women's liberation. For a brief moment, identity politics told women to work on their own issues, but then an identity politics directing people to fight for their own liberation morphed into an intersectionality politics directing people to understand what 'their own' issues were in increasingly narrow ways, which led to the splintering off of doubly and triply oppressed groups. Even where the

104   Moving Forward with Non-Partisan Feminism

wider groups remained functional, there entered a new sense of the more important issues: the issues facing those who are the most oppressed, understood as having the greatest number of identity-generated oppressions. This is captured well in a paper by the feminist philosophers Carol Quinn and Rosemary Tong in 2003:

> we disagree with [the] claim that it is permissible 'to focus on lesser forms of discrimination when greater forms [are] still being practised'. In fact, as we see it, one of the messages of Third Wave feminism, attentive as it is to the differences (race, ethnicity, class, religion, education level, sexual preference, marital status, health status) that exist among women, particularly between women in developed nations and women in developing nations, is that it is not permissible to focus as much feminist energy on getting more women promoted to full professor in Harvard University's philosophy department, say, as on securing a basic education for girls in regimes such as the one the Taliban maintained in Afghanistan.[1]

The political philosopher John Rawls wrote the massively influential *A Theory of Justice* in 1971, popularizing, at least among academics, the principle of 'prioritarianism' – giving priority to the least well off. Still, he meant something quite specific: that when it comes to distributive justice, meaning the distribution of resources across society, *departures from equality are justified when they are to the benefit of the least well off.* That is to say, if a government could either give every citizen a basic income of AU$2,000 per month, or it could fix the minimum wage and un/underemployment benefits to guarantee citizens AU$3,000 per month and otherwise put resources into small businesses and industry so that everyone has an opportunity to earn a lot more, the prioritarian principle would justify the latter. The former gives everyone (and therefore gives the least well off) AU$2,000, the latter gives the least well off

AU\$3,000. Economic inequality on this arrangement is more advantageous to the least well off than economic equality is.

A version of this thinking can justify what Quinn and Tong are saying: in thinking about how to distribute the resources of feminist activism, departures from equality (here meaning projects that benefit *all* women) are justified when they are to the benefit of the least well off, meaning that the least well-off women would get more out of them than they would have got out of the *for all women* activism. Quinn and Tong are probably right about basic education for girls taking priority over sex equality in the academic professoriate, at least assuming there are viable ways for feminist activists in countries like the United States to actually work for girls' educational rights under Taliban rule.

But it's one thing to say that given a feminist concern for women, we should prioritize the issues that affect the least well-off women (understanding 'priority' in the technical way just described), and another to say that, given a group of women, we should prioritize the issues that affect the least well-off *people*, who happen to be women. The latter may be issues that women have in common with men, and which do not disproportionately affect women. The difference is in whether feminism is being conceived as a movement for women's interests (equality, self-determination, liberation, non-domination – I'll just say 'interests' as shorthand in the rest of the chapter) *as women*, or a movement for women's interests *as people*.[2] Quinn and Tong say that 'Third Wave feminism' is 'attentive . . . to the differences (race, ethnicity, class, religion, education level, sexual preference, marital status, health status) that exist among women'.[3] But if your feminist attempt to prioritize the issues of the least well-off women takes you to issues that are not feminist issues, or are not genuinely intersectional issues (issues at the intersection of sex and another aspect of identity where that intersection creates a novel form of oppression), then you are not applying prioritarianism within feminism,

106   Moving Forward with Non-Partisan Feminism

rather you are not doing feminism at all. Instead of applying a sensible moral principle within feminism, you have simply changed the subject. A lot of what goes under the name 'feminism' today has little to do with women; it is global justice by another name. We must return to the idea of women as a class, meaning women *as women*. Consider the following, from the 1968 essay by Beverly Jones and Judith Brown (mentioned already in chapter 2):

> There is something horribly repugnant in the picture of women performing the same menial chores all day, having almost interchangeable conversations with their children, engaging in standard television arguments with their husbands, and then in the late hours of the night, each agonizing over what is considered her personal lot, her personal relationship, her personal problem. If women lack self-confidence, there seems no limit to their egotism. And unmarried women cannot in all honesty say their lives are in much greater measure distinct from each other's. *We are a class, we are oppressed as a class, and we each respond within the limits allowed us as members of that oppressed class.* Purposely divided from each other, each of us is ruled by one or more men for the benefit of all men. There is no personal escape, no personal salvation, no personal solution. The first step, then, is to accept our plight as a common plight, to see other women as a reflection of ourselves, without obscuring, of course, the very real differences intelligence, temperament, age, education, and background create.[4]

Feminism is work for women. It is not work for people, some of whom happen to be women. Advocating for more social housing or a universal basic income or more lenient prison sentencing doesn't make you a *feminist*. These projects might all be good for everyone, but that something is good for everyone doesn't make it feminist. 'Team left' activism isn't feminism because 'team left' activism (like 'team right'

Moving Forward with Non-Partisan Feminism 107

activism) is for everyone, and feminism isn't. This is not to slip from a broad and intentionally pluralistic definition of feminism into defence of a specific *type* of feminism. Recall my definition from the end of chapter 1:

> *Feminist*: a person who works for women's equality (whether of outcome or of opportunity), women's individual self-determination, women's liberation or women's interests (as the person understands them, whether or not that is also as they are); or who works against male dominance.

The socialist feminist is not excluded by this definition because the socialist feminist (if she really is one) works for women's interests. The socialist (whether she calls herself a feminist or not) might be excluded if she *only* works on projects that are good for everyone. We can work for women and prioritize the worst-off women without slipping into working for people and prioritizing the worst-off people but calling that 'feminism'. That's not to say people should not work on the 'everyone' projects, but it is to say they're being misleading when they present that as *feminist* work.

As Jones and Brown noted, women have a 'common plight'. We are a class. That class contains women from across the political spectrum. It makes absolutely no sense to say that a movement in the interests of all women can be fought only by 'team left' women on 'team left' women's terms. That would be like the Black liberationists saying that the movement for Black liberation could be fought only by Black Christians on Black Christians' terms. Or that the fight for lesbian, gay and bisexual rights could only be fought by tertiary-educated gays on tertiary-educated gays' terms.

If minority groups do not owe each other adherence to a particular viewpoint, then minority-group liberation projects cannot be controlled by those with a particular viewpoint – no matter how frequent it is that they are.[5] If 'team left' feminists

108 Moving Forward with Non-Partisan Feminism

care more about 'team left' than about women, that is their prerogative: they should make that clear to other feminists by calling themselves existing terms like 'socialist feminists' or 'Marxist feminists', or adopting a new term like 'left-prioritizing feminist', 'Labour feminist', 'Greens feminist', and so on. They should give *women*-prioritizing feminists every opportunity to avoid working with them, given their different and potentially conflicting priorities.

Once we acknowledge that women from anywhere on the political spectrum can be feminists, and that making a moral/ political distinction reveals there to be far fewer women we must not work with than previously imagined, the question of strategic alliances becomes much clearer. When should any of us work with someone whose priority is not women (as women)? What if we know that a woman works both for women and for a political team, but she puts her team first? For all the loud proclamations that feminists should not work with the right, there is a real question of whether feminists should work with the left, in the specific form of *left-prioritizing feminists*, because when there is a tension between what is good for women and what is good for 'team left', the left-prioritizing woman will choose 'team left'. (And similarly, right-prioritizing feminists will choose 'team right'.) Many cases will not be this clear-cut; maybe someone's priorities are not fully clear even to themselves, or they think that different projects are fully compatible when they are not, because they have not yet faced a hard choice between them.

Let's take up a real example of a potential strategic – or unstrategic! – alliance that left-prioritizing feminists would likely object to.[6] That is the example of controversial Australian Senator Pauline Hanson, who has in recent years supported gender-critical feminist campaigning in Australia (for one example, attending the Let Women Speak event in Canberra in 2023).[7] Most recently, she attempted to introduce a bill that would reinstate the biological definitions of 'man' and 'woman' to Australia's Sex Discrimination Act.[8]

Hanson was elected as the Independent Member for Oxley in Brisbane, Queensland, in 1996, and founded the Australian political party Pauline Hanson's One Nation in the following year. In her first speech to the House of Representatives in 1996, she commented on the 'reverse racism' of special provisions for Aboriginal Australians and argued for government taking what we might today describe as a 'colour-blind' approach to disadvantage. She also said, 'I and most Australians want our immigration policy radically reviewed, and that of multiculturalism abolished'.[9] And on that theme, in what came to be the most notorious part of the speech:

> I believe we are in danger of being swamped by Asians. Between 1984 and 1995, 40% of all migrants into this country were of Asian origin. They have their own culture and religion, form ghettoes, and do not assimilate. Of course I will be called racist, but if I can invite who I want into my home, then I should have the right to have a say in who comes into my country. A truly multicultural country can never be strong or united, and the world is full of failed and tragic examples.[10]

(For the record, and in order to be fair to Hanson in presenting what are now 28-year-old remarks, here is a more recent perspective. In an interview with *60 Minutes Australia* in 2019, Hanson told reporter Liz Hayes, 'I don't go out there just to, you know, set the world on fire, that's not the case . . . I don't intentionally do that, Liz, it's just the way that it . . . comes out sometimes.' When Hayes asked if there's anything in particular she has regretted, Hanson replied, 'Well, I suppose if I hadn't have said "swamped by Asians" in my maiden speech, it might have been different. Because it wasn't meant to offend the Asians that are here, or people who have come here for a new way of life'.)[11]

110   Moving Forward with Non-Partisan Feminism

Let's start with the current One Nation policies of most relevance to all or most types of feminists. On abortion, One Nation is 'pro-life' and 'will seek every opportunity to roll back brutal and extreme abortion law so that both unborn babies and pregnant women will have a level of legal and medical protection once again'. Its more finely specified commitments are less severe than this broad statement makes them sound, however: they are *reducing* the gestational limits for abortion (not banning abortion outright), opposing in particular abortion being legal up to birth; reinstating conscientious objection for doctors who do not want to perform abortions; prohibiting sex-selective abortions; and mandating medical care for babies born alive during an abortion.[12] Under its Family Law and Child Support policy, it 'strongly supports the implementation of a fairer child support system whereby the children are financially supported, not the ex-partner'.[13] (How such a system could possibly be implemented it does not say.)

Now to the policies that will be of relevance to at least some types of feminists, if not all.[14] Under its COVID-19 policy, One Nation opposes mandatory vaccination.[15] Under its World Organisations and Trade Agreements policy, it takes a position against 'Free Trade Agreements that function against the best interest of Australians' and notes that import tariffs should be 'reimplemented on select countries to protect Australia's remaining industry and manufacturing while safeguarding homegrown jobs and wage levels'.[16] Under its Refugees policy, it states a commitment to reducing Australia's refugee intake in order to 'redirect critical funding to Australian services' and supports Australia's withdrawal from the United Nations' 1951 Refugee Convention.[17] And finally, under its Immigration policy, it has a 'zero-net migration policy' focusing on 'permitting only highly skilled migrants from culturally cohesive countries into Australia', noting also that 'Education courses in Australian universities should not be used as a backdoor to immigrate to Australia'.[18]

Moving Forward with Non-Partisan Feminism   111

Should feminists work with Pauline Hanson on the set of projects currently of interest to them? We know from chapter 1 that there's no general answer to this question because people with very different projects can all count as feminists, and their different projects and the contexts in which they pursue them will create different reasons to work or not work with Hanson. Feminists across the board should be in agreement with Hanson about a prohibition of sex-selective abortions; but that is just one point of agreement where there might be many points of disagreement. Mainstream feminists tend to be intersectional and trans inclusive, they may reasonably suspect that her opposition to multiculturalism suggests she will not champion the specifically intersectional interests of non-Aboriginal and non-white women in Australia,[19] and they are likely to disagree with Hanson's aim of amending the Sex Discrimination Act. They appear to have no positive strategic reason *to* work with her and more than one reason *not* to. Christian feminists (depending on the denomination) might agree with Hanson's positions on abortion and trans issues but feel that her positions on immigrants and refugees do not show the compassion and care for the poor that their faith requires. They will have to decide whether that is a serious enough failure to make it unstrategic for them to work with her. They might judge that they can work with her on the issues they agree about and against her on the issues they disagree about without any real tension.

In chapter 3, I mentioned Kathleen Stock referring in an interview to 'people who have strong views about immigration' as being among those that feminists might do better not to work with. Must feminists be pro-immigration? If they must, that would provide *some* reason for them not to work with Hanson. (I say *some* because if there is no real chance of One Nation becoming a major party, then it is not as though working with Hanson really risks her immigration policy being taken up as Australia's national policy. We don't generally refuse to work

112   Moving Forward with Non-Partisan Feminism

with people just because they're wrong about something.) Australian immigration policy affects women both inside and outside of Australia. Does it have distinctive or disproportionate effects on women? It's only a feminist issue if it does. (So if it doesn't, it's not a feminist issue, and the answer to whether feminists must be pro-immigration is 'no'.) If Australia's immigration policy will see the entry of high numbers of young men, some proportion of whom will then perpetrate sexual offences against Australian women, then that immigration policy is an issue for feminists. If Australia's immigration policy will put pressure on social services for the poorest people, and this will have a disproportionate impact on women because women are overrepresented among Australia's poorest people, then that immigration policy is an issue for feminists.

In thinking about whether immigration is a feminist issue, we come up against questions as yet unresolved by political philosophers about what priority it is permissible to give to our fellow countrymen as opposed to 'outsiders'.[20] The resolution of that issue would affect the balance of feminist reasons for and against immigration and foreign aid. If we must give equal concern to all women globally, then surely we must, as feminists, support either immigration or foreign aid (or both) – at least, the immigration entry *of women* and the foreign aid support *for women* as it relates to *women's issues as women*. (Immigration and foreign aid are alternative responses to the same problem, which is that of difficulties faced by persons in their own countries.) Hanson is against immigration (including of refugees), but the One Nation website does not declare a position on foreign aid. *If* she supports foreign aid, then one objection feminists might have had for refusing to work with her, namely that this would lend support to a programme that is bad for women globally, disappears. And if the feminists in each country prioritize the interests of women in their own country, conceived perhaps as an efficient division of labour between countries, then it is not necessarily the case that a

Moving Forward with Non-Partisan Feminism   113

feminist must support either or both immigration and foreign aid.

Even once we settle whether a priority to 'insiders' is permissible, the difficult questions do not end. Given Hanson's history of remarks that have seen opponents brand her as a racist, whether she is in fact a racist or not, are feminists working with her on *anything* risking an accusation of racism that they cannot afford? After all, feminism is for all women, and most women are women of colour. Feminists have an interest in being able to attract a broad base of support, and that will be harder if they are accused of being racists on the grounds that they are willing to 'turn a blind eye' to the racism of someone they are working with. (This is not to concede that race is a feminist issue but to note that many people disapprove of racism.)

There is also the consideration that Hanson is vilified by the parties 'of the left', including Labor and the Greens. (For one vivid illustration, consider how the Australian Greens' Whip Nick McKim speaks about her in parliament when she attempts to introduce the bill to amend the Sex Discrimination Act: 'we have seen her build her grifting political career on demonizing sections of our community'; 'demonization and bigotry'; 'gutter politics').[21] On the other hand, women in politics have an extremely rough time, and we should be careful about letting the vitriol of political opponents mark a political figure as permanently 'toxic'. That would be to give in to a sort of emotional blackmail, where effective political actors can be knocked out by the weight of negative public opinion which may be entirely manufactured. It is perfectly possible that the strategic thing for a feminist to do – especially a feminist who wants to signal that she *stands for women* – is to *refuse* to accept 'team left' political men's contempt for Hanson, to work with her precisely *because* they tell us not to.

I have been asking what strategic reasons feminists of all types/any type have to work, or not to work, with Hanson.

114   Moving Forward with Non-Partisan Feminism

But what about gender-critical feminists in particular? It's for them that the question is most salient, given that Hanson is *already* making contributions towards some of their goals. Should gender-critical feminists work with Pauline Hanson on the set of projects currently of interest to them, including opposition to sex self-identification laws, opposition to conversion therapy laws prohibiting the conversion of gender identity,[22] and pursuit of amendments to federal and state anti-discrimination law clarifying that permanent exemptions for single-sex services also apply to gender identity?[23]

I asked one of the Melbourne gender-critical feminists (it is worth emphasizing that gender-critical feminism, unlike at least some other types of feminism, is deliberately non-partisan) whether she disagreed with any of One Nation's policies. She said, 'I do agree with most of their policies, including [on] immigration and refugees', and, 'can't love Pauline's World Orgs and Trade Agreements policy enough!' But she didn't like the Family Law and Child Support policy, pointing out that the person receiving child support is the one doing the hard work of raising the child, and that many people pay childcare workers. In fact, she called it 'the most petty policy I read in their lineup of policies'. That is just one woman, but I mention her to make the point that if some women in our non-partisan feminist movement agree with most of Hanson's policies, it makes it a lot less obvious that *they*, at least, shouldn't work with her.

What reasons could an opponent of a strategic alliance between Australian gender-critical feminists and Pauline Hanson give to persuade us that this alliance is ill advised? They might say that such an alliance will help Hanson more than the gender-critical feminists, rehabilitating her image by associating her with feminism; or will hurt the gender-critical feminists regardless of what it does for Hanson, associating them with racism and nationalism. But opponents of such an alliance need to do more than just *say* that; they need to establish that it is true. These should not just be treated as rhetorical questions, as though their answers are obvious. Their answers are not obvious. It is also worth noting that people around the world *found it credible* that there was a gender-critical feminist–neo-Nazi alliance in 2023, so these objections to working together with Hanson may be based on delusions about the standing we have to lose. Gender-critical feminists see biological sex as crucial to the 'common condition' that makes women a class, and makes coherent any conception of what women's inequality, other-determination or domination consists in, and what women's liberation or the realization of women's interests might look like. If this is a political, and not merely moral, disagreement with other types of feminists (and with non-feminists), then our 'way of life' requires the legal recognition of sex, and our friends are those who can help us to get it recognized and our enemies are those who want it superseded by gender identity. Hanson is one of the very few politicians in all of Australia who would count as a friend to gender-critical feminists, at least on that single issue. (That does not preclude our thinking about the other issues we care about, both in the shorter term and in the longer term, and considering whether working with Hanson *on* the reinstatement of biological sex to law is likely to lead to us getting less of what we want overall.)

Some gender-critical feminists working with Hanson might actually serve to reinforce the understanding that gender-critical feminism is non-partisan, attracting women across the political spectrum (or, more accurately, 'across the spectrum of political identifications', following the discussion in chapter 4). The only real danger would come from the extremely unlikely event of *all* gender-critical feminists signing on to the full One Nation policy suite because that would serve to make gender-critical feminism politically partisan. Recognizing this also helps to show that even the loud and antagonistic repudiations of 'the right' by the left-prioritizing gender-critical feminists are playing their part, counter-signalling that *some* gender-critical feminists are staunchly committed to 'team

116   Moving Forward with Non-Partisan Feminism

left' (whatever the specific content of that commitment is for each of them).[24]

What I've said in this section about feminists and Pauline Hanson applies equally to one type of feminist thinking about working with another. My pluralistic definition allows for a lot of disagreement – at the extremes, it countenances male-supremacist feminists. Such feminists might have stronger reasons to refuse to work with sameness feminists than they do to refuse to work with, for example, social progressives about other issues. Thinking in terms of left/right is a poor heuristic for deciding who to work with.

Andrea Dworkin was a radical feminist who understood early on that feminism was not a left/right issue. In her paper, 'Woman-Hating Right and Left', presented at a conference in 1987 and published in the 1990 edited collection *The Sexual Liberals and the Attack on Feminism*, she wrote: 'I think as feminists we have a way of looking at problems that other people appear not to understand. To name names, the right and the left appear not to understand what it is that feminists are trying to do.'[25] The left at the time admitted the problem but denied its importance; the right denied the problem.[26] Feminists 'try to understand how we are going to fight male power',[27] and both the left and the right uphold male power in different ways:

> The right wing will promise you a husband whom – yes, it's true, you have to obey him, but then he has to love you for doing it, for obeying him. Now, there are circumstances – like the ones we live under – in which for a lot of women that's not a bad offer. Because you cut down the number of men you have to listen to by several million.
>
> And the left says – and they think this is a good deal – they say . . . to us – 'Well, what we'll do is that we will allow you to have an abortion right as long as you remain sexually accessible to us. And if you withdraw that accessibility and start talking

Moving Forward with Non-Partisan Feminism 117

this crap about an autonomous women's movement, we will collapse any support that we have ever given you: monetary, political, social, anything we have ever given you for the right to abortion. Because if your abortion right is not going to mean sexual accessibility for us, girls, you can't have it.' And that's what they've been doing to us for the last fifteen years.[28]

Feminism targets male supremacy, and men from across the political spectrum believe in male supremacy, they just differ as to its source: 'God or nature'. As Dworkin put it, 'God is the right; nature is the left.'[29] Left-wing men will talk about evolution and innate sex differences; right-wing men will talk about God's creation of men and women as different and complementary.

Resisting male power *requires* bringing women in to feminism, including 'women you have nothing in common with. It means active, proselytizing dialogue with women of many different political viewpoints because their lives are worth what your life is worth. That's why. We have to go past the conventional political barriers, the lines that the men have drawn for us'.[30] Dworkin says that it suits men to segregate women by politics because 'if the girls on either side talked to the girls on the other side, they might just find out that they're being screwed the same way by the same kinds of men'.[31] One of her examples in the paper is of men from *both* left and right working 'to keep women subordinated through . . . pornography'.[32] The right used obscenity laws to 'keep pornography a secret from women but to keep it available to men'.[33] Obscenity laws told pornographers what *not* to do so that their porn would remain available.[34] Left-wing men provided 'socially redeeming material' that met the standards set by the right-wing men.[35] And so:

you have this extraordinary social agreement between the right and the left – who act as if they're fighting all the time – that in fact they can put any amount of woman-hating exploitation, torture, viciousness, or savagery in their magazines, just so they wrap it in a piece of writing that will meet the standard the Supreme Court set. That's all they have to do. They barely have to be literate to meet that standard. And they do this together. And if you let them distract you by the public cockfight they're always having, you miss the fact that when it comes to producing the social product called pornography, they agree.[36]

Left-wing men also, Dworkin says, talk a big game about 'the free market of ideas', and mean, in the end, women. 'They mean women being objectified in pornography, being used in pornography, being exploited in pornography. That's the "free market of ideas". And the ideas look strangely like us. We're the ideas, and they've got a free market in us, folks. And they *do* have a free market in us.'[37] Both the right and the left want women to accept the status quo.[38] She concludes: 'I would like to see in this movement a return to what I call primitive feminism. It's very simple. It means that when something hurts women, feminists are against it. The hatred of women hurts women. Pornography is the hatred of women. Pornography hurts women. Feminists are against it, not for it.'[39]

Dworkin's point could be made for more than pornography. *When something hurts women, feminists are against it.* They're not against it only if it fits into 'team left' politics. (The same goes for 'team right' politics.) They're not against it only if 'team left' women are hurt by it. (The same goes for 'team right' women.) Feminism is not political tribe first, women *of* the political tribe second. It is *women first*.

Notes

Preface

1 https://www.heritage.org/event/the-inequality-the-equality-act-concerns-the-left and see discussion at Murphy 2019a.

2 WoLF is an acronym for Women's Liberation Front, a radical feminist organization of which three of the panellists were members.

3 Murphy 2019a.

4 @SabrinnaValisce, 24 March, 11.22 pm (PDT), online at https://x.com/SabrinnaValisce/status/1772147063758659973?s=20. Similarly, Jane Clare Jones, a British feminist with more than 60,000 followers on X, tweeted sarcastically in response to a defence of one of the organizers 'The only people who care about fascists are ideologically purist bitchy feminists who probably deserve a good kicking for caring about fascists', @janeclarejones 24 March 2024, 3.23 pm (PT); https://x.com/janeclarejones/status/1772026437421109362?s=20. This phrase 'ideologically purist . . . feminists' was a reference back to infighting in the previous year, where Jones and some of her ideological allies had opposed considerably more tenuous connections that they nonetheless perceived as being alliances between feminists and the political right, and had met with a substantial backlash from

120 Notes to pp. viii–ix

non-partisan feminists, some of which coalesced under the terming of her and her allies as 'left-purist feminists'.

5 Bindel 2017.

6 Screenshot posted to X but now deleted. My point in mentioning Valisce's claim is not that a woman on the internet is wrong; that would not be worth saying. My point is that many people assume feminism is an exclusively left-wing project, and yet the reasoning behind this assumption, if there is any, is never made explicit. Valisce provides just one of many possible illustrations of this point.

7 There is a compilation of articles by journalists for Melbourne newspaper *The Age* here: https://www.theage.com.au/nazis-next -door/ See especially Bachelard 2021 and McKenzie and Tozer 2021.

8 Ilanbey and Carmody 2023.

9 Dossier linked here: https://www.womensforumaustralia.org /the_case_against_john_pesutto_an_overview/ A 'comprehensive rejection of John Pesutto's case against her, prepared with lawyers', by Moira Deeming is here: https://x.com/s_deery/status/1640269299372941313

10 Kolovos 2024a; Smethurst, Carmody and Eddie 2024. As I finalize this book, the defamation case *Deeming v Pesutto* is in its second week.

11 Or more precisely, from someone who had been asked by someone else, who had come to support the event, to bring the speaker that she knew he had with him elsewhere. From an interview in the *Guardian*, 'Trihey said that, before he addressed Saturday's rally, he had been holding a separate "information rally and flyer drop off" when he was asked by a member of his group if he could bring his PA system to the parliament. "I was happy to help out as I support what they are doing and so offered them my PA and did a quick intro and closing statement," he said' (Kolovos 2024b). There is, then, at least a one-way relationship of ideological support and material assistance running from the National Workers Alliance to the Women Will Speak event in

Notes to pp. ix–3

this particular instance. (And if allowing Trihey to open and close the event counts as sharing a platform with him, then there is a reciprocal relationship, however brief.)

12 I'm basing my description of events in this sentence and the last on a conversation I had with one of the event organizers, Michelle Uriarau, in March 2024.

13 E.g., @janeclarejones, 25 March 2024, 1.39 am (PDT), online at https://x.com/janeclarejones/status/1772181600077221972?s=20

14 https://x.com/Aja02537920/status/1797572409182359601

15 https://ajasaurus.substack.com/p/ive-been-driven-out

16 UnHerd 2022a.

Chapter 1 Who Is a Feminist?

1 Another equally compelling example would have been the suffragette Christabel Pankhurst, clearly a feminist and yet running on a right-wing political platform. See discussion in Gullace 2014 and chapter 3.

2 Schlafly 2003: 93.

3 Felsenthal 1981: 277.

4 There is more discussion of liberalism and its relation to feminism, especially radical and gender-critical feminism, in my *Gender-Critical Feminism* (2022a: ch. 9).

5 For a discussion of feminism in conservative Catholic, Orthodox Jewish and Evangelical Protestant communities, see Manning 1999.

6 On this point, I follow the discussion in Ferracioli and Terlazzo (unpublished), discussed in some detail in Lawford-Smith and Tuckwell 2024, where we apply the same idea to the concept of allyship. Requiring actual work excludes the person with sincere beliefs and the corresponding dispositions to act on them who – nonetheless – never in fact acts on them, perhaps due to bad luck. That is a cost, but I think worth paying for a definition that is empirically tractable (it's easy to see who is doing the work; it's hard to distinguish those with sincere beliefs and the

122   Notes to pp. 3–11

corresponding dispositions from those who are merely paying lip service to feminist ideals).

7 @UN_Women, 5 January 2019, 12.35 am PDT, online at https://twitter.com/UN_Women/status/1081469111975272448?s=20

8 Lawford-Smith 2023a. I've replaced 'woman' with 'person' for reasons I'll explain shortly.

9 Crispin 2017: 13–14.

10 These three ideas are put forward as aspects of a contemporary understanding of patriarchy in Johnson 2014: 37.

11 Johnson 2014; Criado Perez 2019.

12 Lawford-Smith 2022a: 10, 61–2 and 219, n. 87.

13 Lawford-Smith 2023a; Lawford-Smith 2022a.

14 I'm grateful to Kathleen Stock for discussion on this point.

15 See, e.g., Illien 2020; Rosenblum 2020.

16 For a critique of the sameness/difference dichotomy and an argument for moving to thinking in terms of dominance instead, see MacKinnon 1987.

17 The second wave's 'difference feminists' or 'cultural feminists' are today's 'reactionary feminists' or 'sex-realist feminists', although as I understand things there was less of a connection to religion among the second wave's difference feminists.

18 There is discussion in Andrea Dworkin's chapter 'Jews and Homosexuals' in *Right-Wing Women* of a passage in Romans referring to 'the natural use of the woman' (Dworkin 1983: 108, quoting Romans 1: 22–32).

19 Cf. Dworkin 1983, ch. 6, which argues that feminism *must* take a sameness standard, and anything else is 'anti-feminism'.

20 There are many different types of feminism all claiming that same one word. The most recent edition of Rosemary Tong's *Feminist Thought: A More Comprehensive Introduction*, for example, surveys liberal feminism in three different forms corresponding to three different time periods; radical feminism in two forms; Marxist and socialist feminisms; what she calls 'women-of-color feminisms' in three different forms corresponding to three different time periods; global, postcolonial, and transnational

Notes to pp. 12–15 123

feminisms; psychoanalytic feminism; what she calls 'care-focused feminism'; ecofeminism; existentialist, post-structural, and postmodern feminisms; and what she calls 'third-wave and queer feminisms' (Tong 2017). Whether a person is a feminist is a different issue to what type of feminist they are. Once we know that they are a feminist, we can find out more about what kind of work they do. Some of the types of feminism actually take people outside of the 'work for women' I've required in my definitions, for example socialist feminism and Black feminism add in work for the poor and for Black people (whether they are women or not). So long as this work meets the definition that I conclude the chapter with, the person will count as a feminist.

21 For more detail on the question of whether Schlafly was a feminist, and for the article in which I first considered a list of definitions similar to the one above, see Lawford-Smith 2023a.

22 Benatar 2012: 13–14.

23 There is a similar point in Kirkland 2019; see also discussion in Lawford-Smith 2023b.

24 Personal communication, June 2024.

25 Benatar 2012: 14.

26 Benatar 2012: 23, n. 36, citing Morgan 1970: 520.

27 One of many possible examples comes from the Netflix documentary *Victim/Suspect* (2023), which details the four-year investigation by a female journalist into the phenomenon of police arresting sexual assault victims. Police in the United States would lie about evidence (which is legal, a part of popular interrogation methods for suspects, and known as a 'ruse') in order to pressure the women to recant their reports, and then arrest them for making false reports. The journalist 'took the woman's side' in not taking media reports of women making false rape accusations at face value and looking further into what was going on with the police investigations to create these outcomes.

28 It is perhaps worth adding to the end of this definition the words 'non-derivatively', so that a feminist is a person who works *for women*, not merely a person who works *for people*, from which

124   Notes to p. 16

it follows that the person works for women because women are people. The socialist would thereby work for women (derivatively) but not be a feminist, while the socialist-feminist (at least those with a dual-systems analysis) would be a feminist. An alternative route to the same outcome would be to build into the definition *why* the person works for women, for example, '*Feminist*: a person who has a diagnosis of women's common condition and believes that it is unjust (unequal, unfair, etc.); has a vision of the solution to that condition (or at least a minimum sense of what would help); and who intentionally works for . . .' (then the rest of the definition as I gave it). The challenge for this type of definition is that it cedes empirical tractability because where it is relatively easy to see who's doing what kind of work, it's relatively difficult to establish who has what beliefs and intentions. An advantage, however, is that it would knock out 'accidental feminists', like the men of South Australia who in 1894 attempted to thwart women's enfranchisement by adding to the bill that women could also occupy political office, but whose plan backfired and resulted in women getting both rights. See more at https://www.nma.gov.au/defining-moments/resources /womens-suffrage

29   Roxanne Dunbar writes in an essay 'Slavery' in *No More Fun and Games* (1968a) that 'The Black Revolutionary Movement posits the most advanced revolutionary analysis that this society has produced since Lysander Spooner proposed guerrilla warfare by Slaves, Freedmen, and Poor Whites against the Master Class (North and South). It is true revolutionary analysis which has the potential of curing if acted upon. *Or if it is used in a counter-revolutionary way (Black Nationalism without Socialism and Female Liberation), it can help neutralize one particular problem (racial barriers to the goods) and leave the class system and patriarchy intact*' (p. 5 of archived PDF; my emphasis). There is an assumption here that it would not be okay to work on 'one particular problem' rather than all problems at once. If it were true that one could expect to make just as much progress, at just

the same cost to oneself, by working on all problems at once rather than one particular problem, then I think the assumption would be justified. But it strikes me as unlikely that these two conditions would be met in many real cases. Thus I do not think this gives us a vindication of feminism as exclusively left wing because committedly anti *all* oppression.

30 UnHerd 2022a.

Chapter 2 The 1960s: Feminists Leaving the Left

1 Jones and Brown 1968: 17.
2 Gorska, Kulicka and Jemielniak 2023.
3 Hayden and King 1966 [1965]: 35.
4 Ibid.
5 Ibid.: 36. There is a partial explanation for this apparent hopelessness, which is that Hayden was profoundly inspired by the work of Albert Camus, and so thought that what was important to meaningful action within an authentic life was to refuse complicity in oppression, not to act only when there is some reasonable chance of success. Even if the fight against oppression is Sisyphean, it is nonetheless the thing we should do. See further discussion in Smith 2015: esp. 363 and 371.
6 Hayden and King 1966 [1965]: 36.
7 The SNCC initially had a 'woman-friendly culture', but this turned over time. See discussion in Smith 2015: 373–8.
8 Hayden was born 'Sandra Cason'. She married Tom Hayden in 1961, and soon after became known as Casey Hayden – Smith gives no explanation for the change of first name (Smith 2015: 369). Smith refers to her variously throughout his chapter as 'Cason', 'Casey' and 'Hayden'; I'll stick with 'Hayden' to avoid confusion.
9 Smith 2015: 362–3.
10 Ibid.: 364.
11 Ibid.: 368.
12 Ibid.: 370.
13 Ibid.: 362–3.

126 Notes to pp. 20–24

14 Ibid.: 372.
15 Ibid.: 372; see also Hayden 1988: 107.
16 Ibid.: 372.
17 Ibid.
18 Reprinted in *Notes from the Second Year* in 1970.
19 Readers at the time are likely to have known that this was the 'Counter-inaugural demonstration to protest Nixon's inauguration', which was organized by Mobe (see n. 20). There is a more detailed discussion of the event and background context in Echols 2019 [1989]: 113.
20 National Mobilization Committee to end the war in Vietnam; see https://archives.tricolib.brynmawr.edu/resources/scpc-dg-075
21 Willis 1970 [1968]: 56.
22 Female Caucus of Students for a Democratic Society 1967: 4.
23 Ibid.
24 Jones and Brown 1968: 1.
25 Ibid.: 2.
26 Jones and Brown 1968: 3.
27 The Combahee River Collective 1982 [1977]: 16.
28 Jones and Brown 1968: 3.
29 Ibid.: 16.
30 Ibid: 16. Admittedly, 'for all mankind' and 'a world without horrors' sound broader than feminist movement and perhaps closer to the left at the time, which was especially anti-war. So it remains to be seen how 'new' this project actually was, aside from fully bringing women *in* to the existing project.
31 Ibid: 16.
32 Ibid.: 17.
33 Ibid.: 16–18.
34 Roxanne Dunbar also gives this reason:

> Black Liberation analysis has taught us; the truth has hit us in the guts. We have been touched where we hurt. Indians, Chicanos, poor immigrants, poor whites, women had found movements which proposed benefits to be of dubious relevance to our own

Notes to pp. 25–27

plight. Few of us were 'liberal' (educated) enough to sacrifice our own destiny to that of just another power group. We have learned from Black Liberation analysis that we should work on the liberation of our own people. Our people are oppressed throughout the world, even within the Black Liberation Movement. Our people are women. (Dunbar 1968a: 4–5)

This is a point about what these various movements are working for, and how that is emphatically *not* the liberation of women. If 'our people' are women, and 'we should work on the liberation of our own people', then what is needed is a women's movement.

35 Dunbar 1968a: 6.
36 Ibid.: 7.
37 Echols 2019 [1989]: 80.
38 The last sentence continues 'and to bring about the truly total revolution – the establishment of a radical society without oppression'. I'm not sure how to understand this part of her claim, for she surely did not think that women's liberation alone would solve the problems of Black men, or poor men. Perhaps her thought was that women's liberation was the missing piece of the anti-oppression puzzle, so that with the 'male-oriented, male-dominated radical organizations' fighting all other sources of oppression, a separate women's liberation movement would close the gap (Davidica 1968: 45).
39 Ibid.: 45.
40 Ibid: 45.
41 Ibid.: 46.
42 Dunbar 1968b: 67.
43 Ibid: 67.
44 A note for anyone who goes to read Dixon's original essay: she uses the word 'radical' in a way likely to be confusing to the modern ear, namely to refer to *leftist* rather than *radical feminist* women. That is because of a tradition of referring to leftists more generally as 'radicals'. She calls the women that we would now refer to as radical feminists, 'wildcat women' (Dixon 1970).

128 Notes to pp. 27–32

45 Dixon 1970: 31.
46 Ibid.: 27.
47 Ibid.: 28.
48 Ibid.
49 Ibid.
50 Ibid.: 29.
51 Ibid.: 30.
52 Ibid.
53 Ibid.
54 Ibid.
55 Ibid.: 31.
56 Echols comments that 'the new left's insistence that class and race were by far the most serious social divisions and its denigration of women's liberation as a white, middle-class movement, also contributed to radical feminists' tendency to overstate the significance of gender' (Echols 2019 [1989]: 91).
57 Echols 2019 [1989]: 81; citing an interview she conducted of Baxandall.
58 Echols 2019 [1989]: chs 2 and 3. In addition to reviewing the early writings of the women's liberation movement, Echols also interviewed 41 of the women involved (and one man who was the husband of one of the women, where the woman was herself too ill to be interviewed). Ibid.: see especially 20 and 307, n. 77.
59 Ibid.: 136.
60 Atkinson 1974 [1970]: 95.
61 Ibid.
62 Ibid.: 98.
63 Speaking to the impact of the 'Sex and Caste' memo, Smith wrote that it was read aloud at a workshop during the SDS's national conference in 1965, and that this 'precipitated a three-day discussion about women in SDS and the personal humiliations many of them had experienced' (Smith 2015: 382). This is very clearly a coming together over treatment by leftist men. Smith goes on, 'The SDS men's unwillingness to take gender issues seriously led to a full-scale rebellion by SDS women and to the emergence of

the women's liberation movement in 1967' (Smith 2015: 382). This may be closer to an issue with the left as opposed to leftist men: if left projects are seen as distinct from 'gender issues', such that taking women's issues seriously would be a distraction from left projects, then that does force women to choose *between* the left and women's issues.

64 Smuts 1995: 1.

65 Ibid.: 17.

66 Ibid.

67 Ibid.

68 Ibid.: 17–18.

69 Ibid.: 18.

70 Ibid.: 21.

71 Ibid.: 22.

72 Ibid.: 22–3; her in-text references omitted.

73 Ibid.: 23.

74 Andrea Dworkin said scathingly in 1987, 'Equality is no longer a left-wing goal if it has to include women. The left has disavowed equality as a goal. And equality never was a right-wing goal' (Dworkin 1990 [1987]: 36).

75 Smuts 1995: 15.

76 Wright 1995.

Chapter 3 What's Wrong with the Right?

1 https://www.reddit.com/r/AskFeminists/comments/169abyu/why_cant_feminists_be_conservative/

2 There is no mention of the word 'conservative' in the current version of the r/AskFeminists FAQs, which are marked as last revised three years ago. So it's possible that the poster was misattributing the FAQs of a different subreddit to r/AskFeminists. Either way, what matters for my purposes is the question, rather than precisely the cause of it being asked. See https://www.reddit.com/r/AskFeminists/wiki/rulesfaqresources/

3 Murphy 2019b: 17:33–17:56.

4 See discussion in chapter 1.

130 Notes to pp. 43–48

5 UnHerd 2022b, from 00:42:35–00:44.15. In a more recent article, Bindel refers to 'self-professed "feminists" who proudly declared their support for misogynist-in-chief Donald Trump', which suggests that the objection to 'Trump supporters' may not be so much *that* they are right wing as that Trump is a misogynist. But she did not say more in the article about what she sees the tension between supporting Trump and being a feminist consisting in, for example whether it's that *because* he's a misogynist he can be expected to introduce policies bad for women, or whether it's that feminists have an obligation to dissociate from misogynists, and supporting a candidate politically is a form of association, or something else (Bindel 2024).

6 https://prod-cdn-static.gop.com/docs/Resolution_Platform_2020.pdf (p. 36)

7 https://democrats.org/wp-content/uploads/2020/08/2020-Democratic-Party-Platform.pdf (p. 32)

8 https://www.whitehouse.gov/briefing-room/statements-releases/2024/03/22/fact-sheet-house-republicans-endorse-a-national-abortion-ban-with-zero-exceptions-in-latest-budget/

9 https://www.pewresearch.org/short-reads/2022/06/17/a-closer-look-at-republicans-who-favor-legal-abortion-and-democrats-who-oppose-it/

10 https://www.lp.org/ and https://constitutionparty.com/

11 https://www.gp.org/

12 For states and countries that protect against discrimination on the basis of political beliefs, Greta's behaviour may amount to workplace discrimination, but set that aside here.

13 For the argument that these 'global' judgements of a person are sometimes fitting, see Bell 2011.

14 I cannot help but sympathize with the critique that many of those who appear to feel *so* strongly about 'dead babies' have apparently zero interest in ensuring that those babies' lives are worth living once they're not babies anymore (e.g., through adequate social safety nets). This does seem to give the lie to at least

some of the passionate feeling against abortion. A conservative Catholic woman interviewed for Christel Manning's 1999 book *God Gave Us the Right* expresses a thought that is compatible with mine:

> When each woman begins to think that 'my voice is important', she will stand up for what she sees as a real women's issue, the concern for life. That concern includes not only abortion, but 'the death penalty ... the health care issue. There's so many things involved with being pro-life, and to me being a good Catholic means being pro-life in everything, not just abortion. ... if we're not willing to use our resources, time, money, whatever it takes, to give an equal life to all people, then you can't say you're pro-life'. (Manning 1999: 26)

15 Barring some rare exceptions, for example women with birth-related trauma who have involuntary or very hard-to-control reactions to certain sorts of comments about pregnancy, abortion and/or birth.

16 It also doesn't help if the moral disagreement is *about* liberalism, for example if Greta is a liberal but Libby is not.

17 Dworkin 1983: 94–5.

18 Ibid.: 96.

19 Ibid.: 96.

20 Ibid.: 97.

21 Ibid.

22 Ibid.: 98.

23 Ibid.: 99–100.

24 Ibid.: 100.

25 Gullace 2014: 332.

26 Ibid.

27 Ibid.: 333. Also German men: 'That naturalized men of German origin could vote when patriotic women of British blood could not was a highly emotional way of undercutting a franchise based primarily on sex' (ibid.: 334).

132 Notes to pp. 55–64

28 Gullace 2014: 341.

29 Ibid.: 331. Here's some further evidence of their acceptance by the right:

> As radical-right diehard Lord Willoughby de Broke observed in Parliament during a debate over women's suffrage, 'To those who have any misgivings, I would refer ... Mrs. Pankhurst and the Women's Party... [They have] published a very remarkable, and from a Conservative point of view an exceedingly sound, document [for] national policy... [T]herefore, I do not think we need have many misgivings with regard to the actions that will be taken by ... a certain type and quality of women in this country.' (Ibid.: 333, her ellipses and brackets; her in-text references omitted)

Chapter 4 The Myth of Left and Right

1 Lewis and Lewis 2023: 3.
2 Lewis and Lewis 2023.
3 Lewis and Lewis 2023, ch. 1.
4 Ibid.: 3.
5 Andrews 2023.
6 Lewis and Lewis 2023: 26–7; see also 47.
7 Ibid.: 29 and 57.
8 Here I'm drawing on a conversation the authors had with Coleman Hughes for the *Conversations with Coleman* podcast (Hughes 2023).
9 Lewis and Lewis 2023: 26.
10 Ibid.: 27.
11 Ibid.: 27.
12 Ibid.: 33.
13 Ibid.
14 Ibid.; their footnotes omitted.
15 Lewis and Lewis 2023, ch. 4: esp. 44–5.
16 Ibid.: 92–3.
17 Ibid.: 86.
18 Ibid.: 40–1.

Notes to pp. 65–70

19 Murphy 2019b at 31:45.

20 The Radical Notion 2023. For example, Rose Rickford writes 'Feminism is a form of materialist class politics, aimed at changing political, social, and economic structures so that they are no longer based on the appropriation and exploitation of women. The proper use of the term "left-wing" denotes a commitment to materialist class politics. . . . feminism, as a material class analysis, is truly a left-wing critique of society' (Rickford 2023: 6).

21 Here's Lewis and Lewis making the 'sticky ideologues' point in another way, noting that those who subscribe to a specific iteration of an ideology think of those who subscribe to the next as 'imposters': 'Taft conservatives called Goldwater conservatives "imposters" for advocating military interventionism; Goldwater conservatives called Reagan conservatives "imposters" for focusing on religious issues; Reagan conservatives called George W. Bush conservatives "imposters" for promoting big government; and Bush conservatives called Trump conservatives "imposters" for rejecting military interventionism' (Lewis and Lewis 2023: 40).

22 Lewis and Lewis 2023: 36, my emphasis, their footnotes omitted.

23 Ibid.: 103, n. 17.

24 Ibid.: 40.

25 I say 'in ordinary contexts' because there is at least one special context in which 'egg' is used as a racial slur ('white on the outside, yellow on the inside'). See, e.g., http://www.rsdb.org/slur /egg

26 This might be the best explanation of what's going on with the socialist feminists who, in Lewis and Lewis's terms, are 'sticky ideologues' for Marxism and an older version of the left focused on anti-capitalism and reform of class relations.

27 Lewis and Lewis 2023: 88–91.

28 Lewis and Lewis 2023: 88. Minor stylistic adjustments have been made to the text quoted here (namely, moving the comma outside of the quote marks).

134 Notes to pp. 71–76

29 I have always wondered why a left-wing person working with a right-wing person is meant to result in the left-wing person lending legitimacy to the right-wing cause, rather than the right-wing person lending legitimacy to the left-wing cause, and I can't help but suspect that this is a way of thinking about things produced by a strong political bias – carving the world up into the *good* left and the *bad* right. Naturally, the good lends legitimacy to the bad; but once we recognize that 'left' and 'right' are not synonymous with 'good' and 'bad', it becomes correspondingly less clear which of left and right lends legitimacy to the other, and why it can't be that they both lend legitimacy to each other, or neither lends legitimacy to the other.

Chapter 5 Ethical Versus Political Reasons to Not 'Work With'

1 On the rally see, e.g., Acheson 2024. A reviewer notes that whether there was 'working with' in this case depends on whether the purpose of the rally was only *ostensibly* to protest two-tier policing but *actually* to stir up racial tensions. If that were true, then feminists who attended might have inadvertently contributed to that purpose by adding to the rally's numbers, and then there would be 'working with' in the same sense as for the 2024 Women Will Speak event.
2 Hanisch 2006 [1969].
3 Ibid.
4 Ibid.
5 Ibid.
6 Ibid.
7 Ibid.
8 There is an excellent discussion of related issues in 'Episode 43: Do You Need to Live Your Politics?' of the *RedFem* podcast, 25 September 2023. Online at https://podcasts.apple.com/us /podcast/episode-43-do-you-need-to-live-your-politics/id15740 74250?i=1000629120635

Notes to pp. 77–83

9 This type of view is discussed under the heading 'The Desert View' in Isserow 2018: 3103–6.
10 Isserow 2018: 3111–2 and 3114, her emphasis.
11 Ibid.: 3102.
12 Ibid.
13 Ibid.: 3112.
14 Ibid.
15 Ibid.: 3113–14.
16 See, e.g., Burack 2024.
17 Mason 2021: 524.
18 Ibid., her emphasis.
19 Ibid.
20 Ibid.: 527.
21 Ibid.
22 Ibid.: 524.
23 Ibid.: 529.
24 Ibid.: 525.
25 Ibid.: 52.
26 Bell 2005: 80.
27 Ibid.: 83, her emphasis. Compare with resentment or anger, which 'are responses to a perceived *harm or injury*'.
28 Ibid., her emphasis.
29 Ibid.: 84, citing David Hume. Pulling against the second feature, which states that contempt involves an 'unpleasant affective element', Bell also notes that, because of the comparative element, contempt 'also involves what we might term a "positive self-feeling" of the contemptuous' (ibid.). So even while someone experiencing contempt feels negatively towards the target, they also feel positively towards themselves.
30 Bell 2005: 84.
31 Ibid.: 85.
32 Ibid.
33 Ibid.: 81–3.
34 Ibid.: 85.

136   Notes to pp. 84–86

35 Ibid.: 86. This is a standpoint theory claim, about which there is a lot to criticize. For discussion and a sensible – modest – version of the standpoint claim, see Dror 2023.

36 Bell 2005: 86.

37 Ibid.: 87–8.

38 Ibid.: 88.

39 Ibid.: 89.

40 Ibid.: 91.

41 Ibid.: 82.

42 Ibid.: 86.

43 As Cailin O'Connor and James Weatherall discuss in their book *The Misinformation Age* (2019), *that* there are contrarians is not sufficient to establish that there is reasonable disagreement (although they put this point in terms of scientific disagreement and how media platforms should think about the platforming and publicizing of scientific disagreement). Especially when it comes to disagreement among experts on matters of science, we should also pay attention to things like proportion – how many peer-reviewed papers in good journals are there reporting finding X versus finding Y, for example, and allocating space to the two views accordingly. It's not as clear how to translate this approach to moral and political disagreements, where the explanation of who believes what and why is even more complicated, and there is a question about whether *anyone* is an expert (and when there are whole 'bullshit' disciplines pumping out peer-reviewed bullshit).

44 As I finalize this book, the defamation case in Victoria mentioned in the Preface, n. 10, is in progress, and the defence is relying heavily on accusations of 'association', in particular that by associating with two women who had either tweeted intemperately or appeared in selfies or podcasts with bad people, MP Moira Deeming brought the Victorian Liberal Party into disrepute. For more detail see Lawford-Smith 2024a.

45 Brown 2017.

46 https://www.history.com/this-day-in-history/shirley-chisholm-visits-opponent-george-wallace-in-hospital/

Notes to pp. 87–95

47 I take this phrasing from a recent paper by Edmund Flanigan (Flanigan 2023), but the idea shows up much earlier, in particular in Sarah Hoagland's *Lesbian Ethics* (1988), and a paper she wrote summarizing and commenting on some of the ideas from her book in 1992 (Hoagland 1992). I do not know this to be its *earliest* expression, only that it had a clear expression here.

48 Hoagland 1992: 202.

49 Ibid.: 195.

50 There is also discussion of this agency/victim dichotomy in the context of sex work in Ekman 2013.

51 Hoagland 1992: 203.

52 Flanigan's discussion of futile resistance is a little different to Hoagland's because he frames it in terms of the justification for self-defence. The idea is that in order for aggression to be justified, it must be likely to succeed, but there are cases where we are physically aggressed against and stand no chance of success (perhaps because we are physically overpowered). Nonetheless, many people have the intuition that we may fight back. Flanigan considers and rejects a number of possible justifications for this intuition, and instead argues that futile resistance is a form of protest at the unjust treatment we have been subject to. Obviously, the prohibition on working with the right is not a matter of self-defence, so the puzzle Flanigan is attempting to solve is not relevant for us. But the idea of futile resistance as protest is, and it rationalizes feminist disassociation from the right in a similar way to Hoagland (Flanigan 2023).

53 BBC 2017.

54 Pew Research Center 2024.

55 Joel Feinberg defends a similar conclusion, under the section heading 'Cultural change and the martyrdom of the premature' (Feinberg 1985, ch. 8: 47).

56 There is an issue of how to tell when recriminations are genuine disagreements about the wisdom of some or other political alliance, and when they are the moralizing of individuals about others whose views they don't like. There's also the possibility

138   Notes to pp. 97–99

that the moralizing of the individual is presented as a political disagreement as a form of *cover* – they're really moralizing, but they don't want to look like they're moralizing, so they present themselves as making a political argument. To make progress on these questions we need a clear distinction between the moral and the political, which I'm about to turn to.

57 Schmitt 2007 [1932]: 26.
58 Ibid.
59 Ibid.: 27, my emphasis.
60 Ibid.
61 In an interview after the event with fellow white nationalist Blair Cottrell, Thomas Sewell (who organized the action) said, 'When we got there, we actually initially weren't allowed into the rally, I don't know if that's because the police thought we were Antifa, which again I'm sure I'm going to cop criticism for with the optics with the black bloc, but that's just how we're doing things.' The interview is archived here: https://archive.org/details/tom -sewell-blair-cottrell-march-20th-2023 (and this comment is made at 28:11). There is a photograph of the men here: https:// www.9news.com.au/national/neo-nazi-march-victoria-mel bourne/541ae8aa-adf7-4fe5-b80d-0f27ea192300
62 Swastikas are banned in Victoria, and they did not appear with swastikas, which is one reason why they were difficult to identify.
63 In the same interview mentioned in n. 61, Sewell said,

> [T]here was actually two groups of Antifa that came down. The first group ... they were there really early. But the Socialist Alternative ... they actually organized way up at Carlton Gardens, and they came down about an hour later. And they came down as a big group, and they came running, as well, to try to like, scare the TERFs and the conservatives and the Freedom Rally people off. ... They were running, I'm telling you, Blair, they were sprinting. ... When they saw us ... they suddenly grinded to a halt, like Scooby Doo, like their feet couldn't move further

Notes to pp. 99–102

> backwards ... because they realized that there was twenty solid white dudes standing in front of them that weren't running away. ... And there was no police between us and them. And so they stopped about 50 metres out, and waited for the police to catch up to them. (28:33–30:00)

If this is true – that when the second group of protesters arrived there was no police line to prevent them reaching the Let Women Speak attendees – then members of the National Socialist Network likely prevented violence against the event's attendees by preventing the protesters from reaching them. Livestream footage of the events of that day taken by the independent journalist Rukshan Fernando is still available online, and it more or less corroborates Sewell's version of events. There are a *few* police in place behind the National Socialist Network men, but not nearly enough to hold the large group of protesters back. And other police do seem to be behind or alongside the second group of protesters, rather than ahead of them. See https://www.facebook.com/therealrukshan/videos/229529329488872 from 12:51.

64 Trihey told the *Guardian* that he was a member of the Lads Society – the predecessor to the white supremacist National Socialist Network – for less than a year some five years ago, but left due to philosophical differences (Kovolos 2024b).

65 Reframed in Schmitt's terms, it will be moralized mistreatment at the *least serious* end, and (presumably) things like property damage, interpersonal violence and all-out war, at the most serious end. For the latter, think of an invasion of a secular liberal democratic state by a religious state that will certainly implement religious rule in the territory if the invasion is successful.

66 At the start of a talk at the University of Maine, for example, Tomas Bogardus quotes Peter 3:15, 'Always be prepared to give an answer to everyone who asks you to give the reason for the hope that you have. But do this with gentleness and respect' (Capturing Christianity 2024).

140 Notes to pp. 102–109

67 There is some discussion of humility playing this role in Wright and Pölzler 2022.
68 Schmitt seems to accept no limits on the means to our political ends. If we want to resist him in that, while yet maintaining a moral/political distinction, we might introduce side constraints, such as restrictions on the use of violence.

Chapter 6 Moving Forward with Non-Partisan Feminism

1 Quinn and Tong 2003: 239. The '[the]' in line 1 is my replacement, the '[are]' is theirs. I have also omitted their page references.
2 See also discussion in Lawford-Smith 2022a, ch. 7; Lawford-Smith and Phelan 2022.
3 Quinn and Tong 2003: 239.
4 Jones and Brown 1968: 15, my emphasis.
5 See also discussion in Kianpour 2022, 2023.
6 Another useful real case that I could have taken up is the 2019 panel event 'The Inequality of the Equality Act: Concerns from the Left', hosted at the conservative US think tank the Heritage Foundation, and described briefly in the Preface. As Julia Beck (one of the speakers at the event) said in an interview with Meghan Murphy for *Feminist Current*,

> I figured there was more to gain than lose. . . . In just one week, over fifty news articles were published about the panel in mainstream sources. Even left-wing outlets shared what my fellow panelists and I said, despite merciless slander. The coverage was remarkable. . . . Radical feminist critiques of "gender identity" are now in the congressional record, directed to top officials in the current administration and Supreme Court. . . . I played a tiny yet galvanizing role in the greater conversation in which hundreds of thousands of people around the world are now participating. (Murphy 2019a)

7 Borg 2023.
8 One Nation 2024.

Notes to pp. 109–112

9 Hanson 2016 [1996].

10 Ibid.

11 60 Minutes Australia 2019.

12 One Nation 2023.

13 https://www.onenation.org.au/family

14 What I have in mind here is the claim that these policies have disproportionate impacts on women. For example: because women live longer than men, there will be more women than men among old people, and the mandatory vaccination of a community has a protective effect on its old people; or, because in less developed countries women have fewer opportunities, men will tend to be among the most highly skilled and will therefore be disproportionately eligible for immigration to Australia, creating an inequality of opportunity for some of the worst-off women globally.

15 https://www.onenation.org.au/covid

16 https://www.onenation.org.au/trade

17 https://www.onenation.org.au/refugees

18 https://www.onenation.org.au/immigration. The other policies appear to have sex-equal implications so I have not mentioned them specifically, but the full list is here: https://www.onenation .org.au/issues

19 It is clear from various of Hanson's speeches in parliament that she believes white Australians belong in Australia, so her opposition to multiculturalism cannot be a commitment to an exclusively Aboriginal Australian nation. Thus I am interpreting her as wanting equality of treatment between Aboriginal and white Australians (in her maiden speech she objects to there being 'two sets of rules'), and opposing the entry of all other groups (Hanson 2016 [1996]). I have not followed her career closely though, so she may have made other comments at other times that create a different impression.

20 For a survey of some relevant literature as well as a critique of what the author calls 'methodological nationalism' in political philosophy, see Sager 2021.

142 Notes to pp. 113–118

21 Hanson 2024.

22 There is a considerable literature establishing the harms of attempts to convert sexual orientation, but many bills that seek to ban conversion therapy name *both* sexual orientation and gender identity without adequate empirical justification. Critics of trans activism have worried that this locks clinicians into an affirmation-only approach to gender identity, which may not be the best approach for the child (considering that trans identification has high co-morbidities and children especially may not be the best judges of what is going on with them). There's a more detailed discussion in Lawford-Smith 2024b.

23 That is, where it is *not* considered to be discrimination to exclude one (biological) sex (regardless of gender identity) because doing so advances the substantive equality of the other sex, for example in affirmative action hiring policies for women (biological females).

24 There is a slightly greater elaboration of this idea in Lawford-Smith 2022b.

25 Dworkin 1990 [1987]: 28.

26 Ibid.: 28.

27 Ibid.: 28–9.

28 Ibid.: 29.

29 Ibid.: 30.

30 Ibid.: 31.

31 Ibid.: 31.

32 Ibid.: 32.

33 '[W]hat obscenity laws do when they work in a society is that they hide the pornography from women and children' (ibid.: 33).

34 Ibid.: 34.

35 Ibid.

36 Ibid.: 34–5.

37 Ibid.: 38.

38 Ibid.: 39.

39 Ibid.: 40.

References

Acheson, Ian (2024). 'Tommy Robinson and the Truth about Two-Tier Policing'. *The Spectator*, 24 April. Online at https://www.spectator.co.uk/article/tommy-robinson-and-the-truth-about-two-tier-policing/

Andrews, Evan (2023). 'Where Did the Terms "Left Wing" and "Right Wing" Come from?' *History*, 22 August. Online at https://www.history.com/news/how-did-the-political-labels-left-wing-and-right-wing-originate

Atkinson, Ti-Grace (1974 [1970]). *Amazon Odyssey*. New York: Links Books.

Bachelard, Michael (2021). 'What is a Neo-Nazi?' *The Age*, 16 August. Online at https://www.theage.com.au/national/what-is-a-neo-nazi-20210816-p58j5p.html

BBC (2017). 'Why Australia's Same-Sex Marriage Result Was Not a Surprise'. BBC, 16 November. Online at https://www.bbc.com/news/world-australia-42006450

Bell, Macalester (2005). 'A Woman's Scorn: Toward a Feminist Defense of Contempt as a Moral Emotion'. *Hypatia* 20(4): 80–93.

Bell, Macalester (2011). 'Globalist Attitudes and the Fittingness Objection'. *Philosophical Quarterly* 61(244): 451–72.

References

Benatar, David (2012). *The Second Sexism*. Hoboken, NJ: Wiley-Blackwell.

Bindel, Julie (2017). 'My Work as a Prostitute Led Me to Oppose Decriminalisation'. BBC, 1 October. Online at https://www.bbc.com/news/magazine-41349301

Bindel, Julie (2024). 'American Progressives Better Learn What a Feminist Is'. Al Jazeera, 30 May. Online at https://www.aljazeera.com/opinions/2024/5/30/american-progressives-better-learn-what-a-feminist-is

Borg, Rebecca. 2023. '"She Should Be Embarrassed": Peter Dutton Slams Lidia Thorpe's Behaviour at Let Women Speak Event'. news.com.au, 24 March. Online at https://www.news.com.au/national/politics/she-should-be-embarrassed-peter-dutton-slams-lidia-thorpes-behaviour-at-let-women-speak-event/news-story/80e586d6e0949c863b73ef71395e15b4

Brown, Dwayne (2017). 'How One Man Convinced 200 Ku Klux Klan Members to Give Up Their Robes'. NPR, 20 August. Online at https://www.npr.org/2017/08/20/544861933/how-one-man-convinced-200-ku-klux-klan-members-to-give-up-their-robes

Burack, Emily (2024). 'A Complete Timeline of Prince Andrew and Jeffrey Epstein's Friendship'. *Town and Country*, 5 April. Online at https://www.townandcountrymag.com/leisure/arts-and-culture/a60296556/prince-andrew-jeffrey-epstein-relationship-timeline/

Capturing Christianity (2024). 'Brilliant Lecture on S*x and Gender w/ Spicy QandA | Dr. Tomas Bogardus'. YouTube, 4 June. Online at https://www.youtube.com/watch?v=KGYI4sWhAfI

Combahee River Collective, The (1982 [1977]). 'A Black Feminist Statement', in G. Hull, P. Bell Scott and B. Smith (eds), *All the Women Are White, All the Blacks Are Men, but Some of Us Are Brave*, 2nd edn. New York City: The Feminist Press.

Contempt (1963). Film dir. Jean-Luc Godard. Rome Paris Films.

Criado Perez, Caroline (2019). *Invisible Women: Exposing Data Bias in a World Designed by Men*. London: Chatto and Windus.

Crispin, Jessa (2017). *Why I Am Not a Feminist*. Melbourne: Black Inc.

References 145

Davidica, Maureen (1968). 'Women and the Radical Movement'. *No More Fun and Games*. Archived at Reveal Digital. www.jstor.org/stable/community.28041474

Dixon, Marlene (1970). 'On Women's Liberation'.* Radical America IV/2 (February). [*Note: Dixon's essay is titled 'Where Are We Going?' on the magazine's contents page.]

Dror, Lidal (2023). 'Is There an Epistemic Advantage to Being Oppressed?' *Nous* 57(3): 618–40.

Dunbar, Roxanne (1968a). 'Slavery'. *No More Fun and Games*. Archived at Reveal Digital. www.jstor.org/stable/community.28041474

Dunbar, Roxanne (1968b). 'What Is to Be Done?' *No More Fun and Games*. Archived at Reveal Digital. www.jstor.org/stable/community.28041474

Dworkin, Andrea (1983). *Right-Wing Women*. New York: Perigee Books.

Dworkin, Andrea (1990 [1987]). 'Woman-Hating Right and Left', in Dorchen Leinholdt and Janice Raymond (eds), *The Sexual Liberals and the Attack on Feminism*. New York and London: Teachers College Press, pp. 28–40.

Echols, Alice (2019 [1989]). *Daring to Be Bad: Radical Feminism in America 1967–1975*. Minneapolis: University of Minnesota Press.

Ekman, Kajsa Ekis (2013). *Being and Being Bought*. Melbourne: Spinifex.

Feinberg, Joel (1985). *Offense to Others: The Moral Limits of the Criminal Law*. Oxford: Oxford University Press.

Felsenthal, Carol (1981). *The Sweetheart of the Silent Majority*. New York: Doubleday.

Female Caucus of Students for a Democratic Society (1967). 'Liberation of Women'. *New Left Notes* 2(26) (10 July): 4. Archived at https://www.flickr.com/photos/washington_area_spark/49989842312

Ferracioli, Luara and Terlazzo, Rosa (unpublished). 'Is the "Feminism" in "Liberal Feminism" Redundant?'

146 References

Flanigan, Edmund (2023). 'Futile Resistance as Protest'. *Mind* 132(527): 631–58.

Gorska, Anna Maria, Kulicka, Karolina and Jemielniak, Dariusz (2023). 'Men Not Going Their Own Way: A Thick Big Data Analysis of #MGTOW and #Feminism Tweets'. *Feminist Media Studies* 23(9): 3774–92.

Gullace, Nicoletta (2014). 'Christabel Pankhurst and the Smethwick Election: Right-Wing Feminism, the Great War and the Ideology of Consumption'. *Women's History Review* 23(3): 330–46.

Hanisch, Carol (2006 [1969]). 'The Personal Is Political', in 'The Personal Is Political: The Women's Liberation Movement classic with a new explanatory introduction'. Online at https://www.carol hanisch.org/CHwritings/PIP.html

Hanson, Pauline (2016). 'Pauline Hanson Maiden Speech IN FULL, September 10, 1996'. YouTube, 31 August. Online at https://www .youtube.com/watch?v=hkV1PkPj7ZA

Hanson, Pauline (2024). 'Senate Shut Down: Labor and Greens Block Inquiry into Protecting Biological Women's Rights'. YouTube, 19 September. Online at https://www.youtube.com/watch?v= Z15KLPuztkA

Hayden, Casey and King, Mary (1966 [1965]). 'Sex and Caste' (18 November), *Liberation Magazine*, April. Archived at https:// documents.alexanderstreet.com/d/1006932381

Hayden, Tom (1988). *Reunion: A Memoir*. New York: Random House.

Hoagland, Sarah Lucia (1988). *Lesbian Ethics: Toward New Value*. Palo Alto, CA: Institute of Lesbian Studies.

Hoagland, Sarah Lucia (1992). 'Why Lesbian Ethics?' *Hypatia* 7(4): 195–206.

Hughes, Coleman (2023). 'The Myth of Left and Right with Hyrum Lewis and Verlan Lewis'. Conversations with Coleman, YouTube, 19 August. Online at https://www.youtube.com/watch?v=yHv00 9kiIug

Ilanbey, Sumeyya and Carmody, Broede (2023). 'Liberal MPs Vote to Expel Deeming'. *The Age*, 12 May. Online at https://www.theage

References

147

.com.au/politics/victoria/liberal-mps-gather-to-vote-on-deeming-expulsion-20230512-p5d7v5.html

Illien, Noele (2020). 'Swiss to Vote on Paternity Leave: Nice to Have or Essential?' *New York Times*, 25 September. Online at https://www.nytimes.com/2020/09/25/world/europe/switzerland-paternity-leave.html

Isserow, Jessica (2018). 'On Having Bad Persons as Friends'. *Philosophical Studies* 175: 3099–116.

Johnson, Allan (2014). 'Patriarchy, the System', in *The Gender Knot: Unravelling Our Patriarchal Legacy*. Philadelphia: Temple University Press, pp. 26–47.

Jones, Beverly and Brown, Judith (1968). 'Toward a Female Liberation Movement', Gainesville, FL.

Kianpour, Connor (2022). 'The Minority Retort: In Defense of Defection in Marginalized Groups'. *Public Affairs Quarterly* 36(4): 280–311.

Kianpour, Connor (2023). 'The Political Speech Rights of the Tokenized'. *Critical Review of International Social and Political Philosophy*: 1–21.

Kirkland, Katie (2019). 'Feminist Aims and a Trans-Inclusive Definition of "Woman"'. *Feminist Philosophy Quarterly* 5(1): 1–24.

Kolovos, Benita (2024a). 'John Pesutto Expected to Face Court in Moira Deeming Defamation Case in September'. *Guardian*, 1 February. Online at https://www.theguardian.com/australia-news/2024/feb/02/john-pesutto-to-use-honest-opinion-defence-against-defamation-claim-by-moira-deeming

Kolovos, Benita (2024b). 'Self-Described "Nationalist" Speaks at Anti-Trans Rights Rally on Victoria Parliament Steps'. *Guardian*, 25 March. Online at https://www.theguardian.com/australia-news/2024/mar/26/victoria-anti-trans-rally-parliament-neo-nazi-allegations-matthew-trihey-organiser-michelle-uriarau-ntwnfb

Lawford-Smith, Holly (2022a). *Gender-Critical Feminism*. Oxford: Oxford University Press.

148 References

Lawford-Smith, Holly (2022b). 'Trashing and Tribalism in the Gender Wars', in Noell Birondo (ed.), *The Moral Psychology of Hate*. London: Rowman and Littlefield, pp. 207–33.

Lawford-Smith, Holly (2023a). 'Was Phyllis Schlafly a Feminist?' *Fairer Disputations*, 20 October. Online at https://fairerdisputations.org/was-phyllis-schlafly-a-feminist/

Lawford-Smith, Holly (2023b). 'Who Is Feminism for?' *Philosophers' Magazine*, 18 April. Online at https://www.philosophersmag.com/essays/314-who-is-feminism-for

Lawford-Smith, Holly (2024a). 'Mandatory Denunciations and the Case of Deeming *v.* Pesutto'. *Quillette*, 28 September. Online at https://quillette.com/2024/09/26/court-ordered-denunciations-pesutto-kelly-jane-keane-deeming/

Lawford-Smith, Holly (2024b). 'Sexual Orientation and Gender Identity Conversion Therapy: Or, Who Put the "GI" in "SOGI"?' *Journal of Open Inquiry in Behavioural Science*: 1–17.

Lawford-Smith, Holly and Phelan, Kate (2022). 'The Metaphysics of Intersectionality Revisited'. *Journal of Political Philosophy* 30(2): 166–87.

Lawford-Smith, Holly and Tuckwell, William (2024). 'What is an Ally?' *Critical Review of Social and Political Philosophy*: 1–24.

Lewis, Hyrum and Lewis, Verlan (2023). *The Myth of Left and Right*. New York: Oxford University Press.

MacKinnon, Catharine (1987). 'Difference and Dominance', in *Feminism Unmodified: Discourses on Life and Law*. Cambridge, MA: Harvard University Press, pp. 32–45.

MacKinnon, Catharine (1991). 'Pornography as Defamation and Discrimination'. *Boston University Law Review* 71(5): 793–818.

Manning, Christel (1999). *God Gave Us the Right*. New Brunswick, NJ: Rutgers University Press.

Mason, Cathy (2021). 'What's Bad about Friendship with Bad People?' *Canadian Journal of Philosophy* 51(7): 523–34.

McKenzie, Nick and Tozer, Joel (2021). 'Inside Racism HQ: How Home-Grown Neo-Nazis are Plotting a White Revolution'. *The*

References 149

Age, 16 August. Online at https://www.theage.com.au/national/inside-racism-hq-how-home-grown-neo-nazis-are-plotting-a-white-revolution-20210812-p58i3x.html

Morgan, Robin (1970). *Sisterhood is Powerful*. New York: Vintage Books.

Murphy, Meghan (2019a). 'INTERVIEW: Julia Beck on the Equality Act, Sex Self-Identification, and Why She Perseveres in the Face of Controversy'. *Feminist Current*, 24 September.

Murphy, Meghan (2019b). 'Kathleen Stock and Natasha Chart Discuss the Issue of Feminists "Allying with the Right"'. *Feminist Current*, 21 February. Online at https://www.feministcurrent.com/2019/02/21/podcast-kathleen-stock-and-natasha-chart-discuss-the-issue-of-feminists-allying-with-the-right/

O'Connor, Cailin and Weatherall, James (2019). *The Misinformation Age*. New Haven, CT: Yale University Press.

One Nation (2023). 'Pro-Life'. Online at https://www.onenation.org.au/pro-life

One Nation (2024). 'Press Release: New Legislation to Acknowledge Biological Reality', 13 September. Online at https://www.onenation.org.au/press-release-biological-reality-bill

Pew Research Center (2024). 'Broad Public Support for Legal Abortion Persists 2 Years after Dobbs'. Pew Research Center Report, 13 May. Online at https://www.pewresearch.org/politics/2024/05/13/broad-public-support-for-legal-abortion-persists-2-years-after-dobbs/

Quinn, Carol and Tong, Rosemary (2003). 'The Consequences of Taking the Second Sexism Seriously'. *Social Theory and Practice* 29(2): 233–45.

Radical Notion, The (2023). *Gender-Critical Disputes*, Special Issue (February). Online at www.theradicalnotion.org

Rawls, John (1971). *A Theory of Justice*. Cambridge, MA: Harvard University Press.

Rickford, Rose (2023). 'Feminism and Femalism: We Are Not the Same Movement', in *Gender-Critical Disputes*, The Radical Notion (Special Issue), February. Online at www.theradicalnotion.org

150 References

Rosenblum, Darren (2020). 'Mandatory Paternity Leave: The Key to Workplace Equality'. Forbes, 1 October. Online at https://www.forbes.com/sites/darrenrosenblum/2020/10/01/mandatory-paternal-leave-the-key-to-workplace-equality

Sager, Alex (2021). 'Political Philosophy beyond Methodological Nationalism'. *Philosophy Compass* 16(2).

Schlafly, Phyllis (2003). *Feminist Fantasies*. Dallas: Spence Publishing.

Schmitt, Carl (2007 [1932]). *The Concept of the Political*. Chicago: University of Chicago Press.

60 Minutes Australia (2019). 'Please Explain: Australia's Most Controversial Politician Pauline Hanson | 60 Minutes Australia', YouTube, 15 November. Online at https://www.youtube.com/watch?v=3zNgM0BLSYs

Smethurst, Annika, Carmody, Broede and Eddie, Rachel (2024). 'Two More Defamation Cases Could Sink John Pesutto's Leadership'. *The Age*, 16 March. Online at https://www.theage.com.au/politics/victoria/two-more-defamation-cases-could-sink-john-pesutto-s-leadership-20240315-p5fctg.html

Smith, Harold (2015). 'Casey Hayden: Gender and the Origins of SNCC, SDS, and the Women's Liberation Movement', in Elizabeth Hayes Turner, Stephanie Cole and Rebecca Sharpless (eds), *Texas Women: Their Histories, Their Lives*. Athens, GA: University of Georgia Press, pp. 359–88.

Smuts, Barbara (1995). 'The Evolutionary Origins of Patriarchy'. *Human Nature* 6(1): 1–32.

Tong, Rosemary (2017). *Feminist Thought: A More Comprehensive Introduction*, 5th edn. Abingdon: Routledge.

UnHerd (2022a). 'UnHerd Club – Helen Joyce and Julie Bindel: Should TERFs Unite with the Right?' YouTube, 8 December. Online at https://www.youtube.com/watch?v=Ctcm4cS6NvA

UnHerd (2022b). 'UnHerd Live: Where Does Feminism Go Next?' YouTube, 3 February. Online at https://www.youtube.com/watch?v=VU8WFmI_jDk

Victim/Suspect (2023). Film dir. Nancy Schwartzman. Center for Investigative Reporting Studios.

References

Willis, Ellen (1968). 'Women and the Left'. *Guardian*, February; reprinted in *Notes from the Second Year* (1970), pp. 55–6. Archived at https://repository.duke.edu/dc/wlmpc/wlmms01039

Wright, Jennifer and Pölzler, Thomas (2022). 'Should Morality Be Abolished? An Empirical Challenge to the Argument from Intolerance'. *Philosophical Psychology* 35(3): 350–85.

Wright, Lawrence (1995). 'A Prison Therapist Grapples with a Rapist's Release'. *New Yorker*, 27 August. Online at https://www.newyorker.com/magazine/1995/09/04/a-rapists-homecoming